A Laboratory Manual

You are holding a reproduction of an original work that is in the public domain in the United States of America, and possibly other countries. You may freely copy and distribute this work as no entity (individual or corporate) has a copyright on the body of the work. This book may contain prior copyright references, and library stamps (as most of these works were scanned from library copies). These have been scanned and retained as part of the historical artifact.

This book may have occasional imperfections such as missing or blurred pages, poor pictures, errant marks, etc. that were either part of the original artifact, or were introduced by the scanning process. We believe this work is culturally important, and despite the imperfections, have elected to bring it back into print as part of our continuing commitment to the preservation of printed works worldwide. We appreciate your understanding of the imperfections in the preservation process, and hope you enjoy this valuable book.

CONTAINING

DIRECTIONS FOR A COURSE OF EXPERIMENTS IN
GENERAL CHEMISTRY

Systematically Arranged

TO ACCOMPANY
THE AUTHOR'S "ELEMENTS OF CHEMISTRY"

BY

IRA REMSEN

President of the Johns Hopkins University

THIRD EDITION, REVISED AND ENLARGED

NEW YORK
HENRY HOLT AND COMPANY
1905

Copyright, 1889, 1890, 1902,

BY

HENRY HOLT & CO.

ROBERT DRUMMOND, PRINTER, NEW YORK

NOTE FOR TEACHERS.

On comparing the experiments described in this Manual with those described in my "Elements of Chemistry" it will be found that some of the more difficult ones have been omitted here. As many as possible of those omitted should be performed by the teacher in the presence of the class; and the points of importance should be drawn out by questions put to the members of the class. A number of experiments not included in the text-book are also described. To avoid confusion, the experiments are numbered to correspond with those in the "Elements," the additional ones being designated as a, b, etc., as for instance 106a. Afterwards the pupils should write a full account of what they have seen, and draw such conclusions as the experiments may lead to.

THE AUTHOR.

PREFACE TO THE SECOND EDITION.

In this revised edition of the Manual particular attention has been given to the statements of quantities to be used, with the object of helping the teacher and the pupil as much as possible. The new edition differs from the old also in this respect, that it contains a brief, though systematic, course of experiments in qualitative analysis. The author has endeavored to treat this part of the subject rationally, so as to make the work valuable as a mental discipline, and to discourage the purely mechanical work which is too often done under the name of qualitative analysis.

I. R.

PREFACE TO THE THIRD EDITION.

THIS Manual has again been subjected to a thorough revision. In the main it has not been materially changed, but such additions and corrections have been made in it as were necessary to bring it into conformity with the new edition of the "Elements of Chemistry," which has just been prepared.

I take this opportunity to thank Dr. C. E. Waters for his valuable aid in the work.

I. R.

APPARATUS AND CHEMICALS.

For the benefit of those who have no laboratory at command, and who may wish to make arrangements for performing the experiments described in this book, the following lists have been drawn up. In them is included everything necessary to perform the experiments on a small scale. Should it be desired to fit up a room with conveniences for students, the amount of apparatus necessary will depend upon the number of students, but for each individual the expense will be small, as some of the pieces of apparatus, such as the magnet, weights, scales, etc., need not be multiplied. In place of some of the pieces of apparatus described in the book, ordinary kitchen utensils will answer. Thus, for example, instead of the trough for collecting gases, a tin pan or a deep earthenware dish may be used; instead of the water-bath, a stew-pan, fitted with two or three different-sized tin or sheet-iron rings; in place of glass cylinders for working with gases, wide-mouthed cheap bottles; and in place of Woulff's bottles, wide-mouthed bottles fitted with a cork having two holes. In case of need nearly everything necessary can be procured at an ordinary drug store, though nowadays there is no difficulty in getting the simpler forms of chemical apparatus at little cost.

The publishers do not deal in chemicals and apparatus, nor, they may as well say, receive commissions on them. Any orders should be sent direct to the dealers.

Messrs. Eimer & Amend, Nos. 205 to 211 Third Avenue, New York, whom the publishers take the responsibility of recommending as thoroughly reliable, will furnish each of the following articles at the price given.

If several pieces of the apparatus in List No. 1 are taken, a discount of 10 per cent will be made; on a complete set

20 per cent discount will be allowed; on three or more sets, 25 per cent.

A discount of 10 per cent will be given on a complete set of the chemicals, and of 15 per cent on three or more sets.

For a class of 12 three or four times the amount of apparatus included in List No. 1 could be made to answer, particularly if the pupils are not all required to do the same thing at the same time. As there is, however, always more or less breakage of glass- and porcelain-ware, it is well to have extra pieces of all such apparatus on hand.

As regards chemicals, List No. 2 gives quantities required for a class of 12 as nearly as can be estimated. It is better to have somewhat larger quantities, as some of the experiments may have to be repeated a number of times.

For most items less than the whole set, there will have to be a small additional charge for packing. It should be borne in mind, however, that usually the charge for packing one article must be as large as for several. Some articles can, of course, be mailed without any charge for packing.

List No. 1.

A list of apparatus and chemicals necessary for performing all the experiments described in this book.

APPARATUS.

Item	Price
1 Nest Beakers, 1-3	$0 35
1 Jeweller's Blowpipe, 8 in	10
7 Wide-mouth Flint Bottles, two each, 2, 4, 8 oz., and one 32 oz.	40
1 Bunsen Burner with regulator, or 6 oz. glass alcohol lamp, same price	40
1 5-in. U-tube	25
2 doz. Assorted Corks	20
1 Set Cork Borers, 1-6	1 00
1 Nest Hessian Crucibles, "threes"	5
2 1¼-in. Porcelain Crucibles	36
1 25 c.c. Grad. Cylinder	35
1 Deflagrating Spoon	15
1 Dropping-funnel, 50 c. c.	1 00
1 each Evaporating Dish, 2½ and 3½ in.	35
1 Lead Dish, 2 in	12
1 Round File, 5 in	20
1 Triangular File, 5 in	20
1 Pack White Filters, 4 in	13
4 Flasks: one 4 oz., two 8 oz., one 16 oz.	65
1 Steel Forceps	20
2 Funnels, 2½ in	24
2 Funnel Tubes, one 10 in., one 15 in.	$0 25
1 Gas Bottle, 8 oz., with 2-hole R Stopper	30
½ lb. Assorted Glass Tubing, 4-7.	25
½ lb. Assorted Glass Rods	15
2 Sheets each Red and Blue Litmus-paper	20
1 Horseshoe Magnet, 3 in	12
1 Porcelain Mortar and Pestle, 3½ in.	45
1 Piece Platinum Foil, 1 × 1½ in.	1 00
6 in. Medium Platinum Wire	50
1 Plain Retort, 8 oz	22
1 Stoppered Retort, 16 oz	45
3 ft. Rubber Tubing for gas, ¼ in. (Only needed if Bunsen Burner is used.)	39
2 ft. Rubber Tubing (for connections)	20
1 3½ in. Sand Bath	15
1 Hand Scale, with weights	85
1 Test Tube Stand	30
12 Test Tubes, 5 in	30
1 Test Tube Brush	5
1 Test Tube Clamp	15
1 Iron Tripod	30
1 Filter-stand (2 rings)	45
1 Wire Triangle	5
2 2-in Watch-glasses	10

1 Piece Wire Gauze, 6″ × 6″	$0 10
1 Piece Blue Glass, 2″ × 2″	10
1 Piece Ground Glass, thin, 4″ × 4″	6
1 5-in. Water-bath	90
2 Wire Clamp Supports	1 60
	$16 64

CHEMICALS.

4 oz. Acid Acetic, pure (bottle 5 cents extra)	$0 10
4 oz. Acid Arsenious	10
16 oz. " Hydrochloric (bottle 15 cents extra)	10
8 oz. Acid Nitric (bottle 12 cents extra)	10
2 oz. Acid Oxalic	10
16 oz. " Sulphuric (bottle 12 cents extra)	10
1 oz. Acid Tartaric	10
2 oz. Alcohol, for experiments only (bottle 4 cents extra)	10
8 oz. Alum	10
4 oz. Ammon. Chloride	10
8 oz. " Hydrate, concentrated (bottle 10 cents extra)	10
4 oz. Ammon. Nitrate	10
1 oz. Ammonium Oxalate	10
2 oz. Antimony, powdered	10
2 oz. " and Potassium Tartrate	20
2 oz. Barium Chloride	10
4 oz. Calcium Chloride, fused	10
1 oz. " Carbide (bottle 3 cents extra)	10
4 oz. " Sulphate	10
2 oz. Calc Spar	10
4 oz. Carbon Bisulphide (bottle 5 cents extra)	10
8 oz. Animal Charcoal, powdered	10
8 oz. Copper Foil	20
4 oz. " Sulphate	10
1 oz. " Oxide	15
4 oz. Fluor Spar, powdered	10
1 oz. Indigo	10
1 oz. Iodine (bottle 2 cents extra)	30
4 oz. Iron Filings, fine	10
8 oz. " Sulphide	10
4 oz. " Sulphate	10

2 oz. Lead Carbonate	$0 10
4 oz. " Acetate	10
2 oz. " Nitrate	10
1 oz. " Peroxide	10
4 oz. " Sheet	10
2 oz. " Sesquioxide	10
1 oz. Litmus	10
½ dram Magnesium Ribbon	10
1 oz. Magnesium Sulphate	10
1 lb. Manganese Dioxide, powdered	10
2 oz. Mercuric Chloride	15
2 oz. Mercury	15
1 oz. " Red Oxide	10
1 oz. Nutgalls, powdered	10
2 oz. Paraffin	10
1 oz. Phosphorus (bot. 10c. extra)	15
1 dram Potassium	30
2 oz. " Bromide	10
4 oz. " Carbonate (bottle 5 cents extra)	10
4 oz. Potassium Chlorate	10
1 oz. " Chloride	10
1 oz. " Chromate	10
4 oz. " Bichromate	10
2 oz. " Ferrocyanide	10
1 oz. " Ferricyanide	10
4 oz. " Hydrate Sticks (bottle 5 cents extra)	20
1 oz. Potassium Iodide (bottle 5 cents extra)	25
4 oz. Potassium Nitrate	10
2 oz. " Permanganate	10
1 dram Sodium (bot. 3 c. extra)	10
2 oz. Sodium Acetate, fused	10
2 oz. " Bicarbonate	10
4 oz. " Biborate (Borax)	10
4 oz. " Hydrate (bottle 5 cents extra)	20
4 oz. Sodium Nitrate	10
2 oz. " Phosphate	10
4 oz. " Sulphate	10
1 oz. Sol. of Platinum Chloride	75
8 oz. Sulphur, roll	10
4 oz. Tin, granulated	10
16 oz. Zinc, granulated	20
2 oz. " Sulphate	10
	$10 21

List No. 2.

4 oz. Acetic Acid (pure) (bottle 5 cents extra)	$0 10
4 oz. Acid Arsenious	10
6 lbs. Acid Hydrochloric (bottle 25 cents extra)	30
4 lbs. Acid Nitric (bottle 20 cents extra)	48
8 oz. Acid Oxalic	10
9 lbs. Acid Sulphuric (bottle 25 cents extra)	45
2 oz. Acid Tartaric	10

4 oz. Alcohol (bottle 5 cents extra)	$0 15
2 lbs. Alum	15
1 lb. Ammonium Chloride	12
1 lb. Ammon. Hydrate (Conc.) (bottle 15 cents extra)	20
1 lb. Ammon. Nitrate (bottle 10 cents extra)	25
4 oz. Antimony (powd.)	15
2 oz. " and Potassium Tartrate	20

Item	Price
2 lbs. Animal Charcoal	$0 20
4 oz. Ammonium Oxalate	25
2 oz. Barium Chloride	10
8 oz. Calcium Chloride	12
8 oz. " Carbide	
1 lb. " Sulphate	10
8 oz. Calc Spar	15
1 lb. Carbon Bisulphide (bottle 10 cents extra)	20
2 lbs. Copper Foil	1 20
2 oz. " Oxide	20
¼ lb. " Sulphate	10
8 oz. Fluor Spar (powd.)	10
½ lb. Granulated Tin	30
1 oz. Indigo	10
1 oz. Iodine (bottle 2 cents extra)	30
8 oz. Iron Filings	10
8 oz. " Sulphate	10
2 lbs. " Sulphide	30
½ lb. Lead Acetate	10
4 oz. " Carbonate	10
4 oz. " Nitrate	10
2 oz. " Peroxide	15
4 oz. " Sesquioxide	10
1 lb. " Sheet	40
2 oz. Litmus	10
2 lbs. Manganese Dioxide (coarsely granulated)	30
4 oz. Mercuric Chloride	35
8 oz. Mercury	50
4 oz. Mercury Red Oxide	30
1 oz. Nutgalls, powdered	10
4 oz. Phosphorus	$0 45
2 oz. Platinum Chloride (solution)	1 50
2 drams Potassium	50
½ lb. " Bichromate	10
4 oz. " Bromide	15
1 lb. " Carbonate (bottle 10 cents extra)	12
2 lbs. Potassium Chlorate	30
2 oz. " Chloride	15
4 oz. " Chromate	15
4 oz. " Ferricyanide	20
4 oz. " Ferrocyanide	10
½ lb. " Hydrate (bottle 8 cents extra)	30
2 oz. Potassium Iodide	50
½ lb. " Nitrate	10
4 oz. " Permanganate	15
1 lb. Roll Sulphur	10
1 oz. Sodium (bottle 4 cents extra)	25
8 oz. Sodium Acetate (bottle 8 cents extra)	25
½ lb. Sodium Bicarbonate	10
4 oz. " Biborate	10
2 lbs. " Hydrate (sticks)	80
1 lb. " Nitrate	10
4 oz. " Sulphate	10
8 lbs. " Zinc	60
4 oz. Zinc Sulphate	10
	$18 11

LIST OF EXPERIMENTS.

1. Decomposition of sugar by heat.
2. Change of mercuric oxide by heat.
3. Action of hydrochloric acid on calc-spar or marble.
4. Action of nitric acid on copper.
5. Action of sulphuric acid on zinc.
6. Burning magnesium ribbon.
7. Action of nitric acid on tin.
8. Action of tartaric acid on bicarbonate of soda, dry and wet.
9. Action of iron sulphate on potassium ferricyanide, dry and wet.
10. Mechanical mixture (iron-filings and sulphur).
11. Mechanical mixture examined.
12. Effect of heating a mechanical mixture of iron and sulphur.
13. Heating lead in the air.
14. Heating zinc in the air.
15. Heating tin in the air.
16. Heating lead, zinc, and tin protected from the air.
17.
18. } Burning a candle in a closed space.
18a. Filling vessels with a gas by displacing water.
18b. Oxygen from mercuric oxide.
20. Oxygen from potassium chlorate.
21. Oxygen from potassium chlorate and manganese dioxide.
22. Action of oxygen at ordinary temperature.
23. Burning sulphur in oxygen.
24. Burning charcoal in oxygen.
25. Burning phosphorus in oxygen.
26. Burning a steel watch-spring or picture-wire in oxygen.
27. Nitrogen: preparation and properties.
28. Water from wood and from meat.
29. Crystallization of alum, and presence of water of crystallization in the crystals.
30. Water of crystallization in gypsum.
31. Water of crystallization in copper sulphate.
32. Efflorescence as illustrated by sodium sulphate and sodium carbonate.
33. Deliquescence as illustrated by calcium chloride.
35. Decomposition of water by sodium.

37. Preparation and properties of hydrogen.
38. Purification of hydrogen.
39. ⎫
40. ⎬ Lightness of hydrogen.
41. ⎭
42. Burning hydrogen from platinum tip.
43. Hydrogen burns, but does not support combustion.
50. Ammonia from ammonium chloride.
51. Preparation of ammonia.
52. Preparation of nitric acid.
55. Properties of nitric acid.
56. Action of nitric acid on copper.
57. Preparation of nitrous oxide.
58. Properties of nitrous oxide.
59. Preparation of nitric oxide.
60. ⎫
    ⎬ Properties of nitric oxide.
61. ⎭
62. Preparation and properties of chlorine.
63. Burning hydrogen in chlorine.
64. Hydrochloric acid.
65. Hydrochloric acid: preparation and properties.
66. ⎫
    ⎬ Formation of salts.
67. ⎭
68. Bone-black filter.
70. Reduction of copper oxide by charcoal.
71. Reduction of white arsenic by charcoal.
72. Preparation of marsh gas.
73. Preparation of acetylene.
74. Carbon dioxide from the lungs.
75. Carbon dioxide from carbonates.
76. Preparation and properties of carbon dioxide.
77. Formation of carbonates.
78. ⎫
    ⎬ Action of carbon dioxide on lime-water.
79. ⎭
80. Carbon monoxide.
81. Reduction of copper oxide by carbon monoxide.
82. Flames.
83. Bromine from potassium bromide.
84. Action of concentrated sulphuric acid on potassium bromide.
85. Iodine from potassium iodide.
86. ⎫
    ⎬ Iodine: properties.
87. ⎭
88. Action of concentrated sulphuric acid on potassium iodide.
89. Etching by hydrofluoric acid.
90. Distillation of sulphur.
91. ⎫
    ⎬ Crystallization of sulphur.
92. ⎭
93. Action of sulphur on copper.
94. Preparation and properties of hydrogen sulphide.
95. Action of hydrogen sulphide on the solutions of some compounds.

96. Preparation and properties of sulphur dioxide.
97. Bleaching by burning sulphur.
97a and b. Properties of sulphuric acid.
98. Action of phosphorus and iodine.
98a. Phosphoric acid.
99. Arsine.
100. Detection of arsenic by Marsh's method.
101. Detection of arsenic by reduction of oxide.
102.
103. } Stibine.
104. Potassium carbonate from wood-ashes.
105. Decomposition of water by potassium.
106. Potassium iodide, examination of.
106a. Preparation of potassium hydroxide.
107. Gunpowder.
108. Action of ammonia on acids.
109. Heating ammonium chloride.
110. Flame-reactions.
110a. Detection of potassium, sodium, and ammonium.
111. Preparation of calcium chloride.
112. Lime-water.
113. Plaster of Paris.
113a. Gypsum.
115. Copper sulphate.
116. Copper oxide and hydroxide.
116a. Detection of copper.
117. Silver nitrate, preparation.
118. Silver chloride, bromide, and iodide.
119. Iron; ferrous chloride; ferric chloride.
120.
121. } Potassium chromate and bichromate.
122. Action of potassium chromate and potassium bichromate on hydrochloric acid.
123. Chromates.
123a. Comparison of sulphates and chromates.
123b. Detection of chromium.
124. Lead-tree.
124a. Action of water on lead; on iron.
125. Red lead.
126. Lead peroxide.
127. Fermentation.
128. Soap.
129. "Temporary hardness."
130. "Permanent hardness."
131. Tannic acid.
132. Chlorides.
133. Nitrates.
134. Sulphates.
135. Carbonates.
136. Sulphides.
How to analyze substances.

137. Study of Group I.
138. Study of Group II.
139. Aluminium.
140. Chromium.
141. Iron.
142. Zinc.
143. Manganese.
144. Separation of elements of Group III.
145. Calcium.
146. Barium.
147. Magnesium.
148. Study of Group VI.
General Directions.
Weights and Measures.

$$CaH_2(CO_3)_2$$
$$CaCO_3 + H_2O + CO_2 =$$
$$NaOH \quad CaO$$
$$CaO + H_2O + Na_2CO_3 =$$

LABORATORY MANUAL.

GENERAL LABORATORY DIRECTIONS.

1. Neatness is one of the first conditions of success in chemical work. *Keep your laboratory desk, as well as all your apparatus, clean.*

2. Provide yourself with a working-apron to protect your clothing.

3. Always have a decent towel available.

4. In observing *use your own eyes.*

5. In describing experiments *use your own words.*

6. In thinking over the results *use your own mind.*

7. An experiment should be repeated as many times as may be necessary to secure accurate work.

8. If the results obtained are not those which you have been led to expect, try in every way you can think of to find out what the matter is. See first whether you have worked *exactly* as directed.

9. After an experiment is finished, write in your note-book in the laboratory an account of what you have done. If you are able to draw any conclusions from what you have seen, state what these conclusions are. Write the description accurately and in as good English as possible. Do not use abbreviations. In referring to chemical substances do not use simply the symbol, but the full name with the symbol after it. Thus, potassium chlorate, $KClO_3$; hydrochloric acid,

HCl. Further, in speaking of chemical substances do not use symbols. For example, do not say, "I poured some H_2SO_4 into an H_2O solution of $BaCl_2$," but say in English what you did.

10. After you have written an account of an experiment have it examined by the teacher before you go on to the next one.

11. Always read before and after an experiment or a set of experiments that part of the text-book in which the experiment or experiments are referred to, and keep reviewing constantly.

12. If an experiment not included in your course is performed by you or by your teacher, write an accurate account of it as if you had yourself performed it, but do not make any statement without entirely satisfactory reasons for making it.

13. In working with gases see that all the joints of your apparatus are tight.

14. In case of fire a moist towel thrown over the flame will generally be sufficient to extinguish it.

15. Acid wounds should first be washed out, and a paste of sodium bicarbonate and water then applied.

16. Burns should be treated with a paste of sodium bicarbonate and water.

EXPERIMENT 1.

Test-tube: sugar.

In a clean *dry* test-tube put enough white sugar to make a layer $\frac{1}{4}$ to $\frac{1}{2}$ inch thick. Hold the tube in the flame of a spirit-lamp or laboratory burner as shown in Fig. 1. Heat until no more fumes are given off.

1. What changes take place?
2. What do you see on the sides of the tube?
3. What is the color and taste of that which remains behind?
4. Does it dissolve in water?
5. Is it sugar?
6. Is the change which has taken place chemical or physical?
7. What caused the change?

Fig. 1.

2 Ag Cu · brom-deposit

3

4

$$C_{12}H_{22}O_{11} + \Delta = 12C + 11H_2O$$
Sugar.

HEAT AND CHEMICAL CHANGE.

EXPERIMENT 2.

Glass tubing ⅜ inch internal diameter; file; mercuric oxide; splinter of wood.

1. From a piece of glass tubing of about ⅜ inch internal diameter cut off a piece about 4 inches long by making a mark across it with a triangular file, and then seizing it with both hands, one on each side of the mark, pulling and at the same time pressing slightly as if to break it. Clean and dry it, and hold one end in the flame of a laboratory burner until it melts together.* During the melting twirl the tube constantly between the finger and thumb so that the heat may act uniformly upon it. After it has cooled down put into it enough red oxide of mercury (mercuric oxide) to form a layer ¼ to ½ inch thick.

2. Heat the tube as in Experiment 1.

What change in color do you notice?

What is deposited on the sides of the tube?

3. During the heating insert into the tube a splinter of wood with a spark on the end.

What follows?

4. Take it out and put it back a few times.

Is there any difference between the burning in the tube and out of it?

What difference?

How do you know that the red substance which you put into the tube has been changed?

Is the change chemical or physical?

What caused the change?

---

* Such a tube is called an *ignition-tube*.

Black
Mercury
Brighter combustion
Two A substance a a gas were
formed.

$HgO = Hg + O$

CONTACT AND CHEMICAL CHANGE.

EXPERIMENT 3.

Small piece of calc-spar or marble; ignition-tube; dilute hydrochloric acid; small porcelain evaporating-dish; water-bath; test-tube.

1. Examine a piece of calc-spar or marble. Notice whether it is hard or soft. Heat a small piece in a glass tube such as used in Experiment 2.

Does it change in any way?

Does it dissolve in water? In order to determine whether a substance is soluble in water or not, boil a small piece with distilled water.* Pour off a few drops of the water on a piece of platinum-foil† or a watch-glass, and heat gently to evaporate the water.

FIG. 2.

If there is anything solid in solution there will be a solid residue left on the foil or watch-glass. If not, there will be nothing left.

2. Knowing now the general properties of the calc-spar or marble you will be able to determine whether it is changed or not. Treat a small piece with dilute hydrochloric acid.

What takes place?

3. After the action has continued for about half a

---

* Rain water may be used instead of distilled water. It is better than ordinary drinking water.

† The expensive metal platinum is much used in chemical laboratories, for the reason that it is not easily changed chemically by heat or by most substances used in the laboratory.

EXPERIMENT 3—(*Continued*).

minute insert a lighted match in the upper part of the tube.

Does the match continue to burn?

Does the substance in the tube burn?

Is the invisible substance in the upper part of the tube ordinary air?

How do you know?

Does the solid substance disappear?

4. In order to tell whether it has been changed chemically, the hydrochloric acid must be got rid of. This can be done by heating it, when it passes off in the form of vapor, just as water does, and then whatever is in solution will remain behind. For this purpose put the solution in a small, clean porcelain evaporating-dish, and put this on a vessel containing boiling water, or a water-bath. The operation should be carried on in a place where there is a good draught, so that the vapors will not collect in the working-room. They are not poisonous, but they are annoying. The arrangement for evaporating is illustrated in Fig. 2.

5. After the liquid has evaporated and the substance in the evaporating-dish is dry, examine it and carefully compare its properties with those of the substance which was put into the test-tube.

Is it the same substance?

Is it hard or soft?

Does it change when heated in a tube?

Is there an appearance of bubbling when hydrochloric acid is poured on it?

Does it dissolve in water?

Does it change when allowed to lie in contact with the air?

CONTACT AND CHEMICAL CHANGE.

Experiment 4.

Test-tube; bit of copper; nitric acid; evaporating-dish; water-bath.

1. Bring together in a test-tube a bit of copper, half the size of a ten-cent piece, and 30 to 40 drops of nitric acid.* Hold the mouth of the tube away from your face and do not inhale the vapors.

What is the appearance of the vapors given off?
What is the appearance of the liquid in the tube?
Does the copper dissolve?

If it does not dissolve completely add a few drops more of the acid. Wait until no more action takes place, and if necessary add a few drops more of the acid.

2. Examine the solution, as in the preceding experiment, and see what has been formed.

What are the properties of the substance found after the liquid has evaporated?

Is it colored?
Is it hard or soft?
Does it change when heated in a tube?
Is it soluble in water?
Does it in any way suggest the copper with which you started?

---

* The acid obtained from the dealers is *concentrated*. For ordinary use this should be *diluted* by mixing it with four times its bulk of rain-water or distilled water. Keep two bottles, one containing *concentrated acid*, the other containing *dilute acid*. In this experiment use moderately dilute acid.

2) a) green powder
   b) ~~g-ttin~~
   c) floval.
   d)
   e)
   f)

$3 Cu + 7 H NO_3 = 3(Cu NO_3)_2 + 2 NO$
$+ 4 H_2O$

$NO + O = NO_2$
Red Gas.

CONTACT AND CHEMICAL CHANGE.

EXPERIMENT 5.

Dilute sulphuric acid; bit of granulated zinc; evaporating-dish; water-bath.

1. Try the action of dilute sulphuric acid on zinc in a test-tube.* An invisible gas will be given off. Hold the thumb loosely over the mouth of the tube, and after a few moments apply a lighted match to the mouth of the tube.

What takes place?

2. After the zinc has disappeared evaporate the solution as before. Carefully compare the properties of the substance left behind with those of zinc.

What differences do you find between them?

---

* In experiments made in test-tubes the quantities to be used are always small. In this experiment, for example, use one or two pieces of granulated zinc of such size that they can conveniently be put in the tube. Then add enough dilute sulphuric acid to cover the zinc. The liquid should form a layer from one to two inches in height.

The sulphuric acid obtained from the dealers is *concentrated*. Prepare enough *dilute acid* to fill, say, a 4-oz. bottle, by pouring the concentrated acid *slowly* into four times its bulk of water. Label the bottle *dilute sulphuric acid*. Use this in Experiment 5.

To dilute ordinary concentrated sulphuric acid with water, the acid should be poured *slowly* into the water while the mixture is constantly stirred. If the water is poured into the acid, the heat evolved at the places where the two liquids come in contact with each other may be so great as to convert the water into steam and cause the strong acid to spatter.

$Zn + H_2SO_4 = ZnSO_4 + 2H_2$ gas.
Zinc Sulphate

$2H + O = H_2O$

K_2O_3, ?.

$KClO_3 + \triangle = KCl + 3O$

EXPERIMENT 6.

Strip of magnesium ribbon; sheet of paper.

Hold the end of a piece of magnesium ribbon about eight inches long in a flame until it takes fire. Then hold it over a sheet of paper, so that the light, white substance which is formed may fall upon the paper. If the paper is dark the product can be seen more easily.

What are the properties of the substance formed?
In what way does it differ from magnesium?

CONTACT AND CHEMICAL CHANGE.

EXPERIMENT 7.

Dry flask of 4-oz. capacity; bit of granulated tin or of pure tin-foil; concentrated nitric acid.

In a small dry flask of about four ounces capacity put a bit of granulated tin or of pure tin-foil. Pour upon it enough concentrated nitric acid to cover it. If no change takes place at first, heat gently.

What evidence have you that change is taking place?

Is there anything in this experiment which suggests Experiment 4?

What is left behind after the action is finished?

Compare the properties of the product with those of tin.

1) A light white powder.
2) Color, ~~[struck]~~
   Mg is a metal.
   MgO is a powder.

2 Mg + O₂ = 2 MgO.

SOLUTION AIDS CHEMICAL ACTION.

$H_2C_4H_4O_6$ **EXPERIMENT 8.** $Na HCO_3$

Dry tartaric acid; dry sodium bicarbonate; test-tubes.

1. Mix together in a dry mortar about a gram of dry tartaric acid and about an equal quantity of dry bicarbonate of soda (sodium bicarbonate).

Do you see any evidence of action?

2. Now dissolve about a gram of tartaric acid in 4–5 cubic centimeters * of water in a test-tube, and about the same quantity of bicarbonate of soda in water in another test-tube. Pour the two solutions together.

What evidence have you now that action takes place?

3. Pour water upon the dry mixture first made.

a) Does action take place?
b) What causes the bubbling?
c) Will a match burn in the gas?
d) In which experiment already performed was a similar gas obtained?

---

* With the aid of the graduated cylinder, learn to judge as nearly as possible the volume of 1, 2, 3, 4, 5, etc., cubic centimeters.

The logical forms

a) Effervescence
b) Gas
c) ?

a) Heating of Mercuric Oxide produces oxygen which aids combustion.

NaHC₄... + H₂... =
Sodium acid tartrate + tartaric acid
    "   bi   "

Na H...
Sodium...

SOLUTION AIDS CHEMICAL ACTION.

EXPERIMENT 9.

Small dry mortar ; dry iron sulphate (green vitriol) ; dry potassium ferricyanide (red prussiate of potash).

1. Mix together in a dry mortar about a gram of dry sulphate of iron (green vitriol) and about a gram of dry ferricyanide of potassium (red prussiate of potash).

Does action take place ? *no*

2. Make a solution of each of the two substances and pour them together in a test-tube.*

What evidence have you that action takes place ?

3. Pour water on the dry mixture.
Does action take place ? *colours D blue*

---

*Use about the same quantities of the substances as directed in Experiment 8.

MECHANICAL MIXTURE.

EXPERIMENT 10.

Powdered roll-sulphur ; fine iron filings ; magnifying-glass or small microscope ; small magnet.

1. Mix two or three grams of powdered roll-sulphur and an equal weight of very fine iron filings in a small dry mortar. Examine a little of the mixture with a microscope or a magnifying-glass.

Can you distinguish the particles of sulphur and those of iron?

2. Pass a small magnet over the mixture.

Are particles of iron drawn out of the mixture?

Has chemical action taken place?

MECHANICAL MIXTURE.

EXPERIMENT 11.

Bisulphide of carbon; powdered roll-sulphur; dry test-tube; iron filings; good-sized watch-glass.

1. Pour two or three cubic centimeters of bisulphide of carbon* on about a gram of powdered roll-sulphur in a dry test-tube.

Does the sulphur dissolve?

2. Treat iron filings in the same way.

Does the iron dissolve?

3. Now treat about half of the mixture prepared in Experiment 10 with three or four times its bulk of bisulphide of carbon. After the sulphur is dissolved pour off the solution in a good-sized watch-glass and let it stand. Examine what is left in the test-tube.

Is it iron?

4. After the liquid has evaporated examine what is left on the watch-glass.

Is it sulphur?

---

* *Caution! Carbon bisulphide or bisulphide of carbon takes fire easily. In working with it keep away from flames.*

EXPERIMENT 12.

Powdered roll-sulphur; filings of wrought-iron or powdered iron; dry test-tube; small dry mortar; magnifying-glass; carbon bisulphide; magnet.

1. Mix three grams of finely powdered roll-sulphur with the same weight of fine wrought-iron filings or powdered iron to be had of the druggist. Put the mixture in a *dry* test-tube. Heat gently and note the changes.

At first the sulphur melts, and may even take fire. But soon the mass begins to glow, and if you take the tube out of the flame the mass will continue to glow. This will soon stop; the mass will grow dark and soon cool down.

2. After the action is over and the tube has cooled down, break it and put the contents in a small dry mortar.

Does the mass look like the mixture of sulphur and iron with which you started?

3. Examine with a microscope or magnifying-glass; with carbon bisulphide; with a magnet.

Compare your observations with those made on the mixture used in the preceding experiment.

Treat a little of the substance with dilute sulphuric acid. Also test a little of the original mixture of iron and sulphur with dilute sulphuric acid.

Notice the odor. What difference do you observe between the two cases?

What conclusions does this experiment lead you to?

iv. #12

a) Very much, but blacker.

Particles of iron enhanced into shiny.

$Fe + S \neq \Delta = FeS$
Iron and while

$$...$$
sulphur

CHEMISTRY OF THE AIR.

EXPERIMENT 13.

Small porcelain crucible; tripod; triangle; bit of lead.

1. In a small porcelain crucible arranged as shown in Fig. 3 put a bit of lead the size of a ten-cent piece. Heat by means of a laboratory burner, and notice the changes which take place. After the lead has melted stir with a thick iron wire while heating. Continue to heat and stir until the substance is no longer liquid.

What is its appearance now?

2. Let it cool.

Is it lead?

What difference is there between the action in this case and in the case of melting ice and cooling the water down again?

Which is chemical action and which physical action? Why?

EXPERIMENT 14.

Small porcelain crucible; tripod; triangle; bit of zinc.

Heat a piece of zinc in the same way as you heated lead in the last experiment.

What changes take place?

EXPERIMENT 15.

Small porcelain crucible; tripod; triangle; bit of tin.

Heat a piece of tin in the same way as the metals were heated in the last two experiments.

What changes take place?

CHEMISTRY OF THE AIR.

EXPERIMENT 16.

Same as for Experiments 13, 14, and 15; together with some borax.

Repeat Experiments 13, 14, and 15, adding in each case enough borax to form a complete cover to the metal after the borax and the metal are melted. Do not stir the substances.

Do the metals melt?

Are they changed to powders?

How do you explain the difference?

Experiment 17.

Large flat cork; bit of candle; vessel with water; bell-jar or wide-mouthed bottle; ground-glass plate.

1. Fix a bit of candle an inch or two in length on a large flat cork or a block of wood. Light the candle and place it with the block on water contained in a pail or some other appropriate vessel. Place over it a good-sized glass vessel, either a wide-mouthed bottle or a fruit-jar, as represented in Fig. 4, so that the

Fig. 4.

candle and cork are in the glass vessel and the mouth of the vessel is beneath the surface of the water. Hold it in this position for a few minutes and observe what takes place.

Does the candle continue to burn?

Is all the air contained in the vessel used up when the candle goes out?

EXPERIMENT 17—(*Continued*).

2. Try the experiment a second time, and when the candle is nearly out raise the glass vessel so that air can get in.

Does this make any difference?
What difference?
What do these experiments prove?

EXPERIMENT 18.

Same apparatus as in Experiment 17; candle on wire, or splinter of wood.

After the candle has gone out place your hand on a ground-glass plate over the mouth of the vessel under water, and turn the vessel mouth upwards. Insert

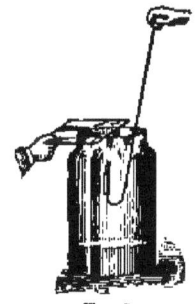

FIG. 5.

into it a lighted candle on a wire or a lighted splinter of wood as shown in Fig. 5.

Is the gas contained in the vessel ordinary air?
How do you know?

COLLECTION OF GASES.

EXPERIMENT 18a.

Bent glass tube as shown in Fig. 6; pneumatic trough or basin nearly full of water; test-tubes.

Gases which are not soluble in water are collected over water. For this purpose the vessel to be filled with the gas is filled with water and turned upside down with the mouth under water, as shown in Fig. 6.

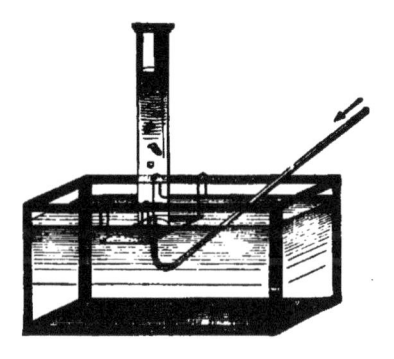

FIG. 6.

The vessels remain filled with water. Why?

2. Try this with test-tubes.

3. Now put the end of a glass tube under the mouth of one of the test-tubes thus filled, and blow gently through it.

What do you notice?

What is in the tube after the water is out of it?

Where did this come from?

OXYGEN.

EXPERIMENT 18b.*

Hard-glass tube arranged as shown in Fig. 7; small glass tube bent as shown in Fig. 7; 2 or 3 grams of mercuric oxide; test-tubes; pneumatic trough.

1. Heat two or three grams of mercuric oxide (red oxide of mercury) in a hard-glass tube arranged as shown in Fig. 7. The tube should be fitted with a good cork with one hole in it through which passes a small glass tube. The end of this smaller glass tube should be bent slightly upward as shown.

What changes take place?

FIG. 7.

2. Collect some of the gas in test-tubes, and by means of a small stick with a spark on it determine whether the gas is ordinary air or not.

Compare this experiment with Experiment 2.

What have you learned from this experiment that you did not learn from Experiment 2?

---

* It was by means of this experiment that oxygen was discovered by Priestley and Scheele in 1774. The discovery was one of the highest importance for chemistry.

OXYGEN.

EXPERIMENT 20.

Flask of 100 c.c. capacity; rubber stopper; bent glass tube; pneumatic trough; cylinders or test-tubes; 2 or 3 grams potassium chlorate.

1. Arrange an apparatus as shown in Fig. 8. *A*

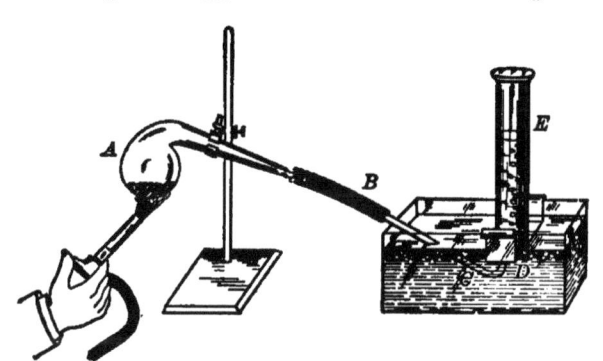

FIG. 8.

represents a retort of about 100 cubic centimeters capacity. *B* is a piece of rubber tubing which is in turn connected with a piece of glass tubing bent upward slightly at the end which is placed under the surface of the water in *C*.

Experiment 20—(*Continued*).

2. In *A* put 2 or 3 grams * (about a sixteenth of an ounce) of potassium chlorate, and gently heat by means of a lamp. Notice carefully what takes place.

3. When gas comes off freely bring the inverted cylinder *E* filled with water over the end *D* of the tube, and let the bubbles of gas rise in the cylinder.

4. In order to examine the gas remove the vessel containing it from the water, first placing over its mouth a glass plate, and then inverting it.

Insert into it a stick with a spark on its end.

What takes place?

Is the gas contained in the vessel ordinary air?

What caused the chemical change in this case?

In what respects is this chemical change like that in the last experiment?

---

* A smaller quantity of potassium chlorate may be used in a test-tube arranged as in Fig. 7.

OXYGEN.

EXPERIMENT 21.

10 grams potassium chlorate; same weight of coarsely powdered manganese dioxide; glass retort; cylinders; bottles.

Mix 10 grams (or about a quarter of an ounce) of potassium chlorate with an equal weight of *coarsely* powdered manganese dioxide* in a mortar. Heat the mixture in a glass retort † arranged as shown in Fig. 8, and collect the gas by displacement of water in appropriate vessels—cylinders, bell-glasses, bottles with wide mouths, etc., using as many as may be necessary to hold the gas given off.

---

*Black oxide of manganese is sometimes adulterated with other substances, and when heated with potassium chlorate it may then give rise to explosions. It should be tested before using by mixing about half a gram of it with an equal weight of potassium chlorate and heating in a dry test-tube. If the decomposition takes place quietly the substance may be used for the preparation of oxygen.

† Instead of a retort a good-sized test-tube may be used. Arrange as in Fig. 7.

EXPERIMENT 22.

Vessels filled with oxygen; deflagrating-spoon; sulphur; charcoal; bit of phosphorus.

Turn three of the bottles containing oxygen with the mouth upward, leaving them covered with glass plates. Into one introduce a little sulphur in a so-called deflagrating-spoon, which is a small cup of iron or brass attached to a stout wire which passes through a round metal plate,* usually of tin (see Fig. 9). In another put a little charcoal (carbon), and in a third a piece of phosphorus† about the size of a pea. Let them stand quietly and notice what changes, if any, take place.

Does oxygen at ordinary temperatures act readily upon the substances used in the experiments?

---

* Such plates can be had of the dealers. One that will answer the purpose can be made by punching a small hole through the centre of the cover of a blacking-box. Force the handle of the spoon through the hole so that it is held firmly in place.

† Phosphorus should be handled with great care. It is always kept under water, usually in the form of sticks. When a piece is wanted, take out a stick with a pair of forceps, and put it under water in an evaporating-dish. *While it is under the water* cut off a piece the size wanted. Take this out by means of a pair of forceps, lay it for a moment on a piece of filter-paper, which will absorb most of the water; then quickly put it in the spoon.

OXYGEN.

EXPERIMENT 23.

Same apparatus as for Experiment 22 ; sulphur.

1. In a deflagrating-spoon set fire to a little sulphur* and let it burn *in the air.* Notice whether it burns with ease or with difficulty. Notice the odor of the fumes which are given off.

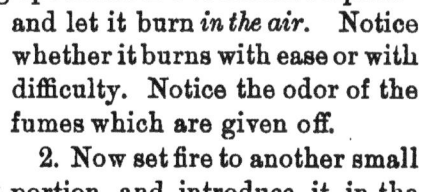

2. Now set fire to another small portion and introduce it in the spoon into one of the vessels containing oxygen, as shown in Fig. 9.

FIG. 9. Does the sulphur burn more readily in the oxygen or in the air?

3. Notice the odor of the fumes given off.

Does it appear to be the same as that given off when the burning takes place in the air?

EXPERIMENT 24.

Same apparatus as for Experiment 22 ; charcoal.

Perform similar experiments with charcoal.
What takes place?
Explain all that you have seen.

---

* Half fill the spoon.

Experiment 25.*

Same apparatus as for Experiment 22 ; phosphorus.

Burn a *small* piece of phosphorus in the air and in oxygen. In the latter case the light emitted from the burning phosphorus is so intense that it is painful to some eyes to look at it. After the burning is over let the vessel stand.

Does it become clear ?

What has taken place ?

---

* It may be as well for the teacher to perform this experiment. It is simple enough, but phosphorus is a dangerous substance, and the burns caused by it heal with difficulty. The piece of phosphorus burned should be about the size of a small pea. It should be put on the deflagrating-spoon, and this should be fixed in the middle of a rather large glass vessel containing oxygen.

EXPERIMENT 26.

Old watch-spring (see foot-note), or iron picture-wire.

Straighten a steel watch-spring* and fasten it in a piece of metal, such as is used for fixing a deflagrating-spoon in an upright position; wind a little thread around the lower end, and dip it in melted sulphur. Set fire to the sulphur, and insert the spring into a vessel containing oxygen.

Instead of the spring iron picture-wire may be used. It is only necessary to heat the end and dip it into powdered sulphur before putting it into the vessel containing the oxygen.

Describe all that takes place.

When iron is exposed to the air what is the color of the substance formed on its surface?

Does this substance suggest anything formed in the experiment?

How do you explain the resemblance?

---

* Old watch-springs can generally be had of any watchmaker or mender for the asking. A spring can be straightened by unrolling it, attaching a weight, and suspending the weight by the spring. The spring is then heated up and down to redness with the flame of a laboratory burner or spirit lamp.

NITROGEN.

EXPERIMENT 27.

Wide-mouthed jar such as used in Experiment 17; small porcelain crucible fastened on a flat cork; bit of candle; trough; sulphur.

1. Place a wide mouthed jar over water in a larger vessel of water. In the middle of a flat cork about three inches in diameter fasten a small porcelain crucible, and float this on the water in the trough. Put in it a piece of phosphorus about twice the size of a pea, and set fire to the phosphorus. Quickly place the jar over it on a support which will prevent the jar from sinking more than an inch or two in the water.

Why is air at first forced out of the vessel?

Why does the water afterward rise in the vessel?

After the burning has stopped and the vessel has cooled down, about what proportion of the air is left in the vessel?

2. Cover the mouth of the jar with a glass plate and turn it mouth upward. Try the effect of introducing one after the other several burning bodies into the gas, as, for example, a candle, a piece of sulphur, etc.

Explain all that you have seen.

WATER.

EXPERIMENT 28.

Dry test-tube ; bit of wood ; bit of fresh meat.

1. In a dry test-tube heat gently a small piece of wood.

What evidence do you obtain that water is given off ?

2. Do the same thing with a piece of fresh meat.

Is water formed in this case?

CRYSTALS AND WATER OF CRYSTAL-LIZATION.

Most substances which dissolve in water are more soluble in hot water than in cold. In a hot solution there may therefore be more of a substance than can remain in solution when cool. On cooling, the substance will in many cases be deposited in regular-shaped masses which are called crystals.

EXPERIMENT 29.

6 to 8 oz. ordinary alum ; funnel and plaited filter ; filter-paper ; dry test-tube.

1. Dissolve some ordinary alum in water (6–8 ounces alum to 200 cubic centimeters of water) by the aid of heat. Filter through a plaited filter and allow the filtered solution to cool.

What takes place ?

2. Pour off the liquid above and place a few of the crystals on a piece of dry filter-paper. After the water is all absorbed from them and they appear dry, put them in a dry test-tube and heat gently.

What evidence have you that water is contained in the crystals ?

. Alum disappears; water becomes cloudy.

2) Crystals of alum precipitate; look like original crystals when dry.
   These crystals become liquid with heat — Efflorescence.

WATER OF CRYSTALLIZATION.

EXPERIMENT 30.

Piece of gypsum; dry test-tube.

In a dry test-tube heat a piece of gypsum the size of a small marble. Gypsum is the natural substance from which "plaster of Paris" is made.

What evidence have you that water is contained in this substance?

What is the appearance of the substance which is left behind after the heating?

Does it resemble the original piece of gypsum?

EXPERIMENT 31.

Few small crystals of copper sulphate; dry test-tube; test-tube; evaporating-dish or small beaker.

1. Heat gently a few small crystals of copper sulphate ("blue vitriol") in a dry test-tube.

What change besides the escape of water do you notice?

What is the color of the powder which is left behind?

2. Dissolve this powder in a little water in a test-tube.

What is the color of this solution?

3. Evaporate off some of the water and let the solution cool. Repeat this, if necessary, until on cooling crystals are deposited.

What is the color of the crystals?

Do these crystals in any way suggest those with which you started?

Ep. 31.

1) Turns from blue to green (bright) then to a white powder (very very white)
2) By By the explosive action of the particles
2 a) Blue-green
3) Crystals are green when damp, and light bluish green when dry. Does not resemble the original. Same is a suggestion of color.

Ep. 30 $CaSO_4 + \Delta$ = {white powder} {Plaster-paris.}

The works form {side of} tube as the heat acts.

8) The powder does not resemble gypsum $CaSO_4$

Na_2SO_4

EFFLORESCENT COMPOUNDS.

EXPERIMENT 32.

Crystals of sodium sulphate and of sodium carbonate; watch-glass.

Select a few crystals of sodium sulphate or Glauber's salt which have not lost their lustre. Put them on a watch-glass, and let them lie exposed to the air for an hour or two.

What evidence have you that change takes place?

Perform a similar experiment with a few clear crystals of sodium carbonate (sal soda or washing soda).

Is there any evidence of change in this case?

DELIQUESCENT COMPOUNDS.

EXPERIMENT 33.

$CaCl_2$

Calcium chloride; watch-glass.

Expose a few pieces (the size of a pea) of calcium chloride to the air. Calcium chloride was the product obtained in Experiment 3. If there is none in the laboratory, make some.

What change takes place when the substance is exposed for some time to the air?

Loses crystal form and becomes a granular powder

Becomes moist

DECOMPOSITION OF WATER.

EXPERIMENT 35.

Sodium; battery-jar or large beaker with water; piece of cardboard.

Throw a small piece of sodium* on water contained in a battery-jar or large beaker. Cover the vessel with a piece of cardboard. While it is floating on the surface apply a lighted match to it.

What takes place?
What causes the flame?
Why is the flame yellow?

---

* The metals sodium and potassium are kept under kerosene oil. When a small piece is wanted, take out one of the larger pieces from the bottle, roughly wipe off the oil with filter-paper, and cut off a piece the size needed. It is not advisable to use a piece larger than a small pea. *Dry your fingers before handling these metals.*

Sodium is active on surface of water.
Flame due to burning hydrogen.
Yellow color is caused by sodium.

HYDROGEN.

EXPERIMENT 37.

Granulated zinc; ordinary hydrochloric acid; cylinder or test-tube; dilute sulphuric acid.

1. In a cylinder or test-tube put a few pieces of *granulated zinc*, and pour upon it enough ordinary hydrochloric acid to cover it.

What do you notice?

2. After the action has continued for a minute or two, apply a lighted match to the mouth of the vessel.

What takes place?

3. Try the same experiments using sulphuric acid which has been diluted with four times its volume of water.*

What is the result?

What is the gas given off?

---

* See note, Experiment 5.

$Zn + 2HCl = 2H + ZnCl_2$

$Zn + H_2SO_4 =$

Violent activity. Gas given off. evidently
White fumes. The gas burns explosively
The action causes considerable heat.

$H_2SO_4 + Zn$
 Very little action; a bubble of gas only once in
a while; more activity with heat. Very
active with $Cu(NO_3)_2$.
 Gives off Hydrogen.

HYDROGEN.

EXPERIMENT 37 *—(*Continued*).

Woulff's flask (Fig. 10) or wide-mouthed bottle (Fig. 11); granulated zinc; dilute sulphuric acid; cylinders and bottles.

For the purpose of collecting hydrogen the gas should be evolved from a bottle with two necks called a Woulff's flask (see Fig. 10), or a wide-mouthed bottle in which is fitted a cork with two holes (see Fig. 11).

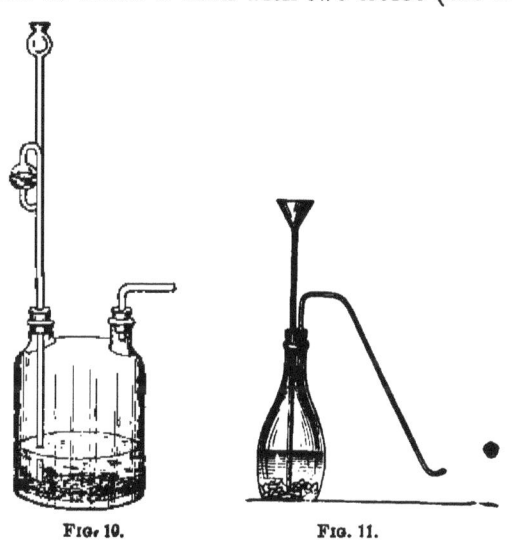

FIG. 10.   FIG. 11.

Put a small handful of granulated zinc † into the

---

* Always be cautious when working with hydrogen. The danger lies in the fact that a mixture of hydrogen and oxygen, or of hydrogen and air, *explodes violently when a spark or flame comes in contact with it.* Always let the gas escape for a time, from 3 to 5 minutes, or longer if the acid acts slowly upon the zinc, and then, before applying a flame to the gas issuing from the generating vessel, fill a test-tube by displacement of water, and light it to see whether it will burn quietly without explosion. If it will not, wait longer.

† Some zinc, particularly that which is pure, does not act readily upon acids. Whether the action is taking place freely or not can be seen by the effervescence in the flask and by the rate at which bubbles

EXPERIMENT 37—(*Continued*).

bottle and pour upon it enough *cooled* dilute sulphuric acid (1 volume concentrated acid to 4 volumes of water) to cover it. Collect by displacement of water as in the case of oxygen. Should the action become slow add a little more of the dilute acid. Fill four or five cylinders and bottles with the gas.

EXPERIMENT 38.

Pass some of the gas through a solution of *potassium permanganate*. Collect some of it, and notice whether it has an odor.

Arrange the apparatus as shown in Fig. 12. The solution of potassium permanganate is contained in the small cylinder *A*, and the tubes are so arranged that the gas bubbles through it.

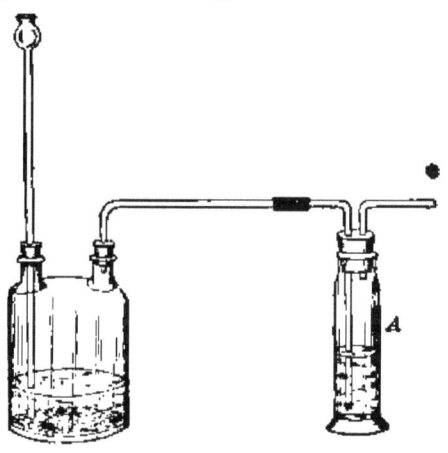

FIG. 12.

of gas appear at the end of the delivery-tube when this is placed under water. If the action is slow, *wait longer* before collecting it and before setting fire to it. It is better not to use zinc which acts slowly.

HYDROGEN.

EXPERIMENT 39.*

Place a vessel containing hydrogen with the mouth upward and uncovered. In a short time examine the gas and see whether it is hydrogen.

EXPERIMENT 40.

Cylinder of hydrogen; empty cylinder.

Gradually bring a vessel containing hydrogen with its mouth upward below an inverted vessel containing air, in the way shown in Fig. 13.

Is there hydrogen in the vessel with the mouth upward?

FIG. 13.

Is there hydrogen in the other vessel?

EXPERIMENT 41.

Soap; clay pipe; hydrogen generator.

Soap-bubbles filled with hydrogen rise in the air. The experiment is best performed by connecting an ordinary clay pipe † by means of a piece of rubber tubing with the exit-tube of a flask in which hydrogen is being generated. Small balloons of collodion are also made for showing the lightness of hydrogen. Large balloons are always filled with hydrogen or some other light gas. Some kinds of illuminating-gas are rich in hydrogen, and may therefore be used for the purpose.

---

* In all experiments with hydrogen see that no flames are burning near you.

† It is best to wet the pipe thoroughly to prevent the loss of hydrogen by diffusion.

HYDROGEN.

EXPERIMENT 42.

Hydrogen generator; platinum tube; glass tube.

Roll up a small piece of platinum-foil, or take a small platinum tube, and fuse it into the end of a glass tube as shown in Fig. 14.

Connect the burner thus made with a hydrogen generator and light the gas. Is the flame colored or colorless?

Hold a piece of wire in it. Is it hot?

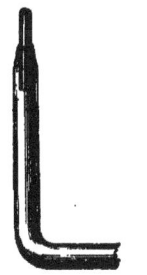

FIG. 14.

EXPERIMENT 43.

Taper fastened on wire; cylinder full of hydrogen.

1. Hold a wide-mouthed bottle or cylinder filled with hydrogen with the mouth downward. Insert into the vessel a lighted taper held on a bent wire, as shown in Fig. 15.

What do you observe?
What burns?
Does the taper continue to burn?

2. Withdraw the taper and hold the wick for a moment in the flame at the mouth of the cylinder, then withdraw it entirely. Put it back again in the hydrogen.

Does hydrogen support combustion?
Does it burn?

FIG. 15.

3. Try similar experiments with a piece of wood.

AMMONIA.

EXPERIMENT 50.

Ammonium chloride ; watch-glass ; caustic soda ; caustic potash ; quicklime.

1. To a little* ammonium chloride on a watch-glass add a few drops of a strong solution of caustic soda, and notice the odor of the gas given off.

2. Do the same thing with caustic potash.

3. Mix a gram of quicklime and a gram of ammonium chloride in a mortar, and notice the odor.

Has ammonium chloride this odor ? - *yes*
What is the substance with the odor ?
How is it formed in the experiments ?

---

*As much as you can lay on a ten-cent piece.

NH

$H_2O + NH_3 + NaCl$

$NH_4Cl + NaOH = \cancel{NH_4 + NaCl + O}$ Ammonia gas

$ H_2O + KCl + NH_3$

$NH_4Cl + KOH = \cancel{NH_4 + KCl + O}$ Ammonia gas stronger than above

$\cancel{CaO + NH_4Cl = NH_4 + CaCl + O}$ strong ammonia gas

$CaO + 2NH_4Cl = 2NH_3 + CaCl_2 + H_2O$

AMMONIA.

EXPERIMENT 51.

Apparatus shown in Fig. 16; 100 grams quicklime; 50 grams ammonium chloride; sand-bath; dry cylinder or bottle, Fig. 17; taper on wire.

1. Arrange an apparatus as shown in Fig. 16, omit-

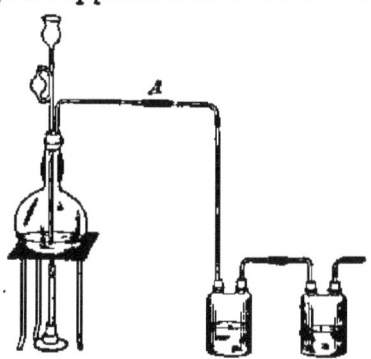

FIG. 16.

ting, however, the funnel-tube. In the flask put 100 grams of quicklime and add just enough water to slake it without making it moist; then add 50 grams ammonium chloride and mix by shaking. Push the stopper into place and gently heat on a sand-bath.* The Woulff's flasks are one-third filled with water, and the tubes so arranged that the gas given off from the generating flask must pass down nearly to the surface of the water, but *not bubble through it.*

After the air is driven out the gas will be completely absorbed by the water in the first flask.

2. After a short time disconnect at *A*, and connect with another tube bent upward. Collect a cylinder

---

*A sand-bath is a shallow vessel of sheet-iron or tin-ware containing a layer of dry and fine sand.

$CaO + NH_4Cl \quad 2NH + 20$

$Ca(OH)_2 + 2NH_4Cl = CaCl_2 + 2NH_3 + 2H_2O$

Ammonium
Ammonia Water.

EXPERIMENT 51—(*Continued.*)

or bottle full of the escaping gas by displacing air, *placing the vessel with the mouth downward*, as the gas is much lighter than air. The arrangement is shown in Fig. 17. The tube through which the gas enters the vessel should pass through a piece of thick paper or of card-board, and this should rest against the mouth of the vessel. The object of this is to prevent currents of air from carrying the gas out of the vessel. You can determine when the vessel is full of gas by the strong smell of the gas. *In working with the gas great care must be taken to avoid breathing it in any quantity.* The vessel in which the gas is collected should be dry, as water absorbs ammonia very readily. Hence also, the gas cannot be collected over water.

FIG. 17.

3. As soon as the cylinder or bottle is full of gas, connect the delivery-tube again with the series of Woulff's flasks, and pass the gas over the water as long as it is given off. Save this liquid and label it *ammonia*. It is this solution which is used under the name ammonia in the laboratory.

4. In the gas which you have collected introduce a burning stick or taper.

Does the gas burn?

Does it support combustion?

EXPERIMENT 52.

Apparatus shown in Fig. 18 ; 25 grams sodium nitrate ; 15 grams concentrated sulphuric acid.

Arrange an apparatus as shown in Fig. 18. In the

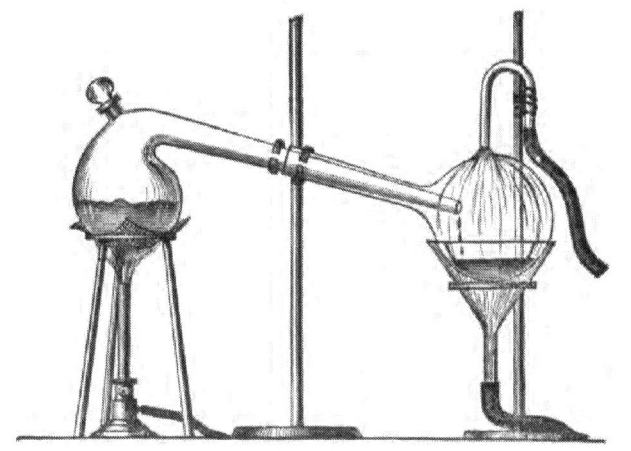

FIG. 18.

retort* put 25 grams sodium nitrate (Chili saltpetre) and 15 grams concentrated sulphuric acid. Heat gently.

What takes place ?

What is the color due to ?

Put this liquid in a bottle and label it "Concentrated Nitric Acid."

---

* This experiment may be simplified by using a large test-tube as a receiver. It can be kept cool by immersing the lower part in cold water contained in an evaporating-dish or beaker.

~~$Na_2NH_3 + H_2SO_4 = He_2SO_4 + NH_4$~~

$2NaNO_3 + H_2SO_4 = Na_2SO_4 + 2HNO_3$

$Na_2SO_4 + KOH$

NITRIC ACID.

EXPERIMENT 55.

Liquid obtained in last experiment ; bits of tin, zinc, iron, lead.

1. In test-tubes try the action of the liquid you obtained in the last experiment on a few small pieces of granulated tin contained in a small flask.

Describe the results obtained.

2. Perform similar experiments with bits of zinc, iron, and lead.

What results do you obtain ?

EXPERIMENT 56.

Copper-foil ; ordinary, commercial concentrated nitric acid ; flask ; evaporating-dish ; water-bath ; dry test-tube ; concentrated sulphuric acid.

1. Dissolve a few pieces (10–20 grams) of copper-foil in ordinary, commercial concentrated nitric acid diluted with about half its volume of water. Add the diluted acid gradually to the copper, so that not much more is used than is necessary to dissolve the metal. The operation should be carried on in a good-sized flask, and either out of doors or under a good hood.

What action takes place ?

After it is over what is the appearance of the liquid in the flask ?

2. Pour it out and evaporate to crystallization.

3. Heat two or three small crystals in a dry test-tube.

What change do you observe ?

4. Treat three or four small crystals with four or five drops of concentrated sulphuric acid, and warm gently.

Do you obtain any evidence that the substance is a nitrate ?

NITROUS OXIDE.

EXPERIMENT 57.

Retort of 3-4 oz. capacity; 10-15 grams crystallized ammonium nitrate; wide rubber tube; cylinders; bottles; candle on wire; bits of wood.

In a retort heat 10 to 15 grams crystallized ammonium nitrate until it has the appearance of boiling. Do not heat higher than is necessary to secure a regular evolution of gas. Connect a wide rubber tube directly with the neck of the retort, and collect two or three bottles full of the gas over water, as in the case of oxygen.

What chemical change takes place?

EXPERIMENT 58.

Cylinders of nitrous oxide; splinter of wood; candle; phosphorus; deflagrating-spoon.

Insert into the gas obtained in the last experiment a piece of burning wood, a candle, and a small bit of phosphorus.

Explain what takes place.

NITRIC OXIDE.

EXPERIMENT 59.

Apparatus shown in Fig. 19; copper-foil; ordinary concentrated nitric acid; cylinders; bottles.

Arrange an apparatus as shown in Fig. 19. In the flask put ten or twelve pieces of copper-foil one or two inches long by about half an inch wide. Cover this with water. Now *slowly* add ordinary concentrated nitric acid. When enough acid has been added gas will be given off. If the acid is added quickly it not infrequently happens that the evolution of gas takes place too rapidly, so that the liquid is forced out of the flask through the funnel-tube. *This can be avoided by not being in a hurry.*

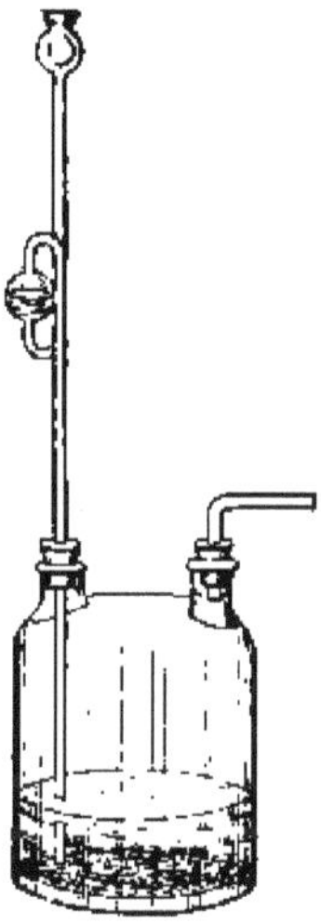

What is the color of the gas in the flask at first?

What is it after the action has continued for a short time?

FIG. 19.

Fill two or three vessels with the gas over water.

Do not inhale the gas. Perform the experiments with nitric oxide where there is a good draught.

NITRIC OXIDE.

EXPERIMENT 60.

Vessels filled with nitric oxide in last experiment; burning candle.

Turn one of the vessels containing colorless nitric oxide with the mouth upward and uncover it.

What takes place?

Explain the appearance of the colored gas in Experiment 59, and the fact that it afterward disappeared.

What was in the vessel at the beginning of the operation?

EXPERIMENT 61.

Cylinder of nitric oxide; candle.

Into one of the vessels containing nitric oxide insert a burning candle.

Does the gas burn? } *no*
Does it support combustion?

Brown – red fumes green

CHLORINE.

EXPERIMENT 62.*

Apparatus shown in Fig. 20; 100 grams (3 to 4 ounces) manganese dioxide; concentrated hydrochloric acid; sand-bath; 6 or 8 dry cylinders; funnel and filter; evaporating-dish; water-bath.

1. In a flask put about 100 grams (3 to 4 ounces) of black oxide of manganese. Pour upon it enough ordinary concentrated hydrochloric acid to cover it completely. Arrange the apparatus as shown in Fig. 20. Heat gently in a sand-bath.

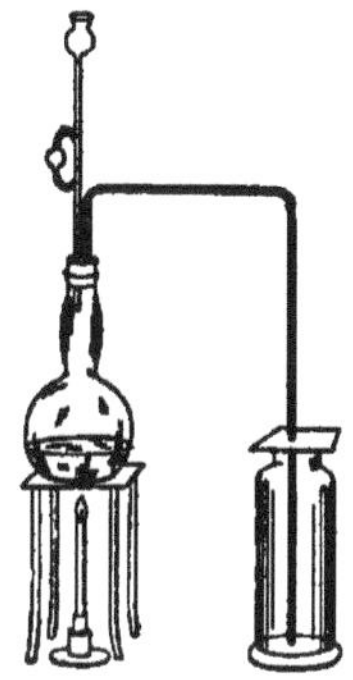

What is given off?

Write the equation representing the action.

2. Fill six or eight *dry* cylinders or bottles with chlorine by letting the delivery-tube extend to the bottom of the collecting vessel and covering the mouth of the vessel with a piece of paper. You can see when the vessel is full by the color of the gas.

FIG. 20.

---

* The experiments with chlorine should be carried on in a place where the draught is good. Do not inhale the gas.

CHLORINE.

EXPERIMENT 62—(*Continued*).

Vessels filled with chlorine; powdered antimony; copper-foil; piece of paper with writing on it; colored flowers; colored calico.

3. Into one of the vessels containing chlorine introduce a little (as much as you can put on a ten-cent piece) finely powdered antimony. If the action does not take place readily, warm the antimony slightly before pouring it into the chlorine.

What takes place?

In what respects is this experiment like the one in which iron was burned in oxygen?

4. Into a second vessel put a few pieces of copper-foil which you have heated.

What takes place?

5. Into a third vessel put a piece of paper with writing on it, some flowers, and some pieces of colored calico which you have *moistened*.

What takes place?

6. Into a fourth vessel put a *dry* piece of the same calico used in 5.

What difference is there in the action of the chlorine on the dry and on the moist calico?

Write a full account of the method you have used in preparing chlorine, and of the results obtained in the experiments with chlorine.

Compare chlorine with hydrogen and with oxygen.

HYDROCHLORIC ACID.

Experiment 63.

Hydrogen generator; cylinder of chlorine; blue litmus* solution.

Light a jet of hydrogen in the air and carefully introduce it into a cylinder of chlorine.

Does it continue to burn?

What is the appearance of the flame?

What evidence have you that a product is formed?

Pour a little blue litmus solution into the cylinder and shake.

What do you notice?

Experiment 64.

Common salt; concentrated sulphuric acid; test-tube.

Pour 2 or 3 cubic centimeters of concentrated sulphuric acid on a gram or two of common salt in a test-tube.

What takes place? *Fumes evolved*

Is a gas given off? — *white gas*

What is its appearance?

---

* Litmus is a vegetable substance prepared for use as a dye.

$$2NaCl + H_2SO_4 = Na_2SO_4 + 2HCl$$

HYDROCHLORIC ACID.

EXPERIMENT 65.

Apparatus shown in Fig. 16; common salt; concentrated sulphuric acid; sand-bath; dry cylinder; candle on wire; funnel and filter; evaporating-dish; water-bath; filter-paper; ignition-tube; test-tubes; iron filings; granulated zinc; manganese dioxide; blue litmus; caustic soda or ammonia.

Arrange an apparatus as shown in Fig. 16, Exp. 51. Weigh out, separately, 100 grams common salt, 100 grams concentrated sulphuric acid, and 20 grams water. Mix the acid and water, taking the usual precautions (see note, Exp. 5). Let the mixture cool down to the ordinary temperature, and then pour it on the salt in the flask.

2. Heat the flask *gently* in a sand-bath. Conduct the gas at first over water contained in two Woulff's flasks.

After the gas has passed for 10 to 15 minutes disconnect at *A* (see Fig. 16).

What appears?

"Blow your breath" on the gas coming out of the tube, taking care not to get too near the end of the tube.

What effect has this?

3. Apply a lighted match to the end of the tube.

Does the gas burn?

Does the match continue to burn?

4. Collect some of the gas in a dry cylinder as in the case of chlorine, and then connect the generating-flask again with the flasks containing the water, and let the action continue until no more gas is given off.

In collecting chlorine and hydrochloric acid the

EXPERIMENT 65—(*Continued*).

vessels must stand mouth upward. Are these gases heavier or lighter than air?

Has the gas any color?

Is it transparent?

Insert a burning stick or candle in the cylinder filled with the gas.

Does the gas support combustion?

5. Express by an equation the action which takes place in the preparation of hydrochloric acid.

What is left in the flask?

After the flask has cooled down pour water on the contents until it is covered 2 or 3 inches deep, and, when the substance is dissolved, filter and evaporate the solution to such a concentration that, on cooling, the sodium sulphate is deposited. Pour off the liquid, and dry the solid substance by placing it upon folds of filter-paper.

6. Compare the substance with the common salt which you put into the flask at the beginning of the experiment.—Heat a small piece of each in a dry tube.—Treat a small piece of each in a test-tube with a little concentrated sulphuric acid.

What differences do you observe between them?

If in the experiment you should recover all the sodium sulphate formed, how much would you get?

7. Put about 20 cubic centimeters of the liquid from the first Woulff's bottle in a porcelain evaporating-dish and heat over a small flame just to boiling.

Is hydrochloric acid given off?

Can all the liquid be driven off by boiling?

8. Try the action of 8–10 cubic centimeters of the

EXPERIMENT 65—(*Continued*).

liquid from the first Woulff's bottle on a gram or two of iron filings in a test-tube.

Is a gas given off?

What is it?

9. Add 8–10 cubic centimeters of the liquid to a gram or two of granulated zinc in a test-tube.

What gas is given off?

10. Add 8–10 cubic centimeters to a gram or two of manganese dioxide in a test-tube. Warm gently.

What is given off?

How do you know?

11. Add ten or twelve drops to 2 or 3 cubic centimeters of water in a clean test-tube. Taste the solution.

How would you describe the taste?

12. Add a drop or two of a solution of blue litmus, or put into it a piece of paper colored blue with litmus.

What change takes place?

13. To the solution to which litmus has been added add a drop or two of caustic soda or ammonia.

What change takes place?

Write a full account of all you have done since you started with the sulphuric acid and common salt, and be sure that your account contains answers to all the questions which have been asked.

NEUTRALIZATION—FORMATION OF SALTS.

EXPERIMENT 66.

Two burettes and stand; beakers; stirring-rod; dilute solutions of sulphuric, hydrochloric, and nitric acids, and of potassium and sodium hydroxides; litmus solution.

1. Make dilute solutions of nitric, hydrochloric, and sulphuric acids by mixing 4 cubic centimeters of dilute acid, such as is used in the laboratory, with about 200 cubic centimeters of water. Make also dilute solutions of caustic soda and caustic potash by dissolving about 1 gram of each in 200 cubic centimeters of water. Keep the solutions in well-corked bottles.

2. Fill one burette with the nitric acid solution and the other with caustic soda. Measure off a definite quantity, say 20 cubic centimeters, of acid, add 2 or 3 drops of litmus solution, and then cautiously add caustic soda from the other burette, stirring constantly until the solution just turns blue. When red it is acid; it becomes blue when it is alkaline. At the turning-point it is neutral. Note the volume of caustic soda used. Repeat with 15 cubic centimeters and 10 cubic centimeters of acid. What relation do the quantities of alkali bear to one another?

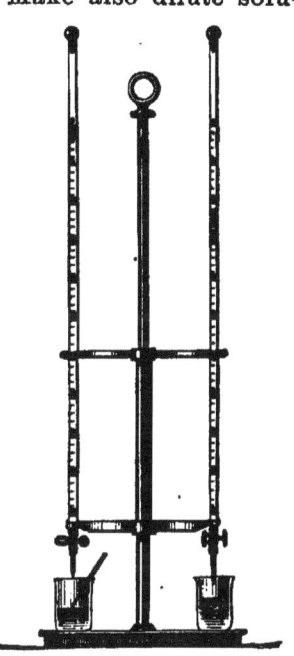

FIG. 21.

EXPERIMENT 66—(*Continued*).

3. Wash out the burette containing the acid and fill it with hydrochloric acid. Carry out the same operation as before.

4. Use also sulphuric acid.

In all these cases what is the relation between the quantities of alkali used with 10, 15, and 20 cubic centimeters of the same acid?

5. Perform similar experiments, using caustic potash and each of the three acids in succession.

NEUTRALIZATION—FORMATION OF SALTS

EXPERIMENT 67.

Caustic soda; hydrochloric acid; litmus solution; evaporating-dish; water-bath; nitric acid; ignition-tubes; sulphuric acid.

1. Dissolve 10 grams caustic soda in 100 cubic centimeters of water. Add dilute hydrochloric acid slowly, examining the solution from time to time by means of a piece of paper colored blue with litmus. As long as the solution is alkaline it will cause no change in the color of the paper The instant it passes the point of neutralization it changes the color of the paper red. When this point is reached, evaporate the water on a water-bath to complete dryness and see what is left. Taste the substance.

Has it an acid taste?

Does it suggest any familiar substance?

If it is common salt or sodium chloride, how ought it to conduct itself when treated with sulphuric acid?

Does it conduct itself in this way?

Is the substance an alkali? Is it an acid? Is it neutral?

Write the equation representing the action.

2. Perform the same experiment as under 1, using dilute nitric acid instead of hydrochloric acid.—Compare the product with sodium nitrate.

Heat a small specimen of each in a tube closed at one end. What takes place?

Treat a small specimen of each with a little sulphuric acid in test-tubes. What takes place?

Write the equation representing the action.

Write an account of the process of neutralization.

EXPERIMENT 67—(*Continued*).

3. Perform a similar experiment with sulphuric acid and caustic soda.

What is formed ? In what other experiments have you obtained this substance ?

Write the equation expressing the action.

4. Try similar experiments with caustic potash and nitric, hydrochloric, and sulphuric acids.

In each case compare the product with some of the same substance from the laboratory bottle.

CHARCOAL.

EXPERIMENT 68.

Funnel 5 to 6 inches in diameter at mouth; filter; bone-black; solution of indigo; ink.

1. Make a filter of bone-black by fitting a paper filter into a funnel 12 to 15 mm. (5 to 6 inches) in diameter at its mouth. Half fill this with bone-black. Pour a dilute solution of indigo * through the filter.

What effect does this have on the color of the solution?

2. Do the same thing with a dilute solution of ink. If the color is not completely removed by one filtering, filter the solutions again.

3. The color can also be removed from solutions by putting some bone-black into them and boiling for a time. Try this with half a liter each of the ink and indigo solutions used in the first part of the experiment. Use about 4 to 5 grams of bone-black in each case. Shake the solutions frequently while heating.

---

* Prepared by treating 1-2 grams of powdered indigo for some time with 4-5 cubic centimeters of warm concentrated sulphuric acid and diluting with a liter of water.

CARBON.

EXPERIMENT 70.

Powdered copper oxide; powdered charcoal; apparatus shown in Fig. 22; lime-water; concentrated nitric acid.

1. Mix together 2 or 3 grams powdered copper oxide, CuO, and an equal bulk of powdered charcoal; heat in a hard-glass tube to which is fitted an outlet tube, as shown in Fig. 22. Pass the gas which is given off into clear lime-water contained in a test-tube.

Is it carbon dioxide?

What evidence have you that oxygen has been extracted from the copper oxide?

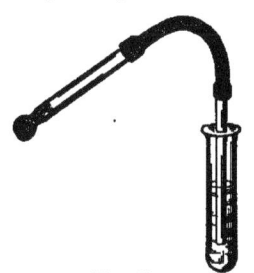

FIG. 22.

What is the appearance of the substance left in the tube?

Does it suggest the metal copper?

2. Treat a little with concentrated nitric acid.

What should take place if the substance is metallic copper? (See Experiment 56.)

What does take place?

What is the reaction which takes place between the copper oxide and the charcoal? Write the equation.

Compare the action of hydrogen with that of carbon on copper oxide.

In what respects are they alike, and in what respects do they differ?

CARBON.

EXPERIMENT 71.

White arsenic; ignition-tube; powdered charcoal.

Perform an experiment like the last with a little *white arsenic* in a small glass tube closed at one end. Take about equal parts of charcoal and arsenic.

Explain what you see.

Compare the action in this case with that in Experiment 70.

MARSH-GAS.

EXPERIMENT 72.

Fused sodium acetate; dry potassium hydroxide; quicklime; retort; cylinders; bottles.

Mix 5 grams fused sodium acetate, 5 grams potassium hydroxide, and 7½ grams quicklime. Heat in a retort. Collect over water as in making nitrous oxide.

Does the gas burn?

Does it give light in burning?

ACETYLENE.

EXPERIMENT 73.

Woulff's flask; dropping-funnel; glass tube; acetylene burner; calcium carbide.

Arrange an apparatus as shown in Fig. 23. Into the flask put a few pieces of calcium carbide.

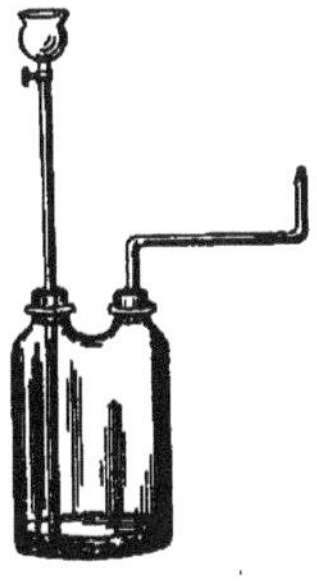

Close the stop-cock in the dropping-funnel and fill the latter with water.

Open the stop-cock slightly so that the water may drip very slowly upon the carbide in the flask.

After the gas has escaped for some time light it.

FIG. 23.

What sort of flame does it give?

Attach an acetylene burner to the end of the outlet-tube and again light the gas.

What difference do you notice? Why?

CARBON DIOXIDE.

EXPERIMENT 74.

Test-tube; glass tube; lime-water.

Blow through some lime-water by means of an apparatus arranged as shown in Fig. 24.

What evidence have you that your lungs give off carbon dioxide?

EXPERIMENT 75.

Sodium carbonate; marble; test-tubes; dilute hydrochloric, sulphuric, nitric, and acetic acids.

FIG. 24.

1. Put about a gram of sodium carbonate in each of four test-tubes; and then add to one tube about 4–5 cubic centimeters of dilute hydrochloric acid, to a second the same quantity of dilute sulphuric acid, to a third the same quantity of dilute nitric acid, and to the fourth the same quantity of dilute acetic acid.

What takes place?

Is a gas given off?

2. Pass it through lime-water. See Exp. 70 for explanation of "pass."

Is it carbon dioxide?

3. Perform the same experiment with small pieces of marble.

What gas is given off?

What conclusions can you draw from these observations?

How can you easily detect carbon dioxide?

CARBON DIOXIDE.

EXPERIMENT 76.

Apparatus shown in Fig. 25; marble; ordinary hydrochloric acid; cylinders; bottles; candle on wire; scales.

1. Arrange an apparatus as shown in Fig. 25. In the flask put some pieces of marble, and pour ordinary hydrochloric acid on it to the depth of about an inch. Collect the gas by displacement of air, placing the vessel with the mouth upward. Fill five or six cylinders or bottles with the gas.

2. Into one introduce a lighted candle, and afterwards a burning stick.

What takes place?

3. With another proceed as if pouring water from it. Pour the invisible gas upon the flame of a burning candle.

4. Pour some of the gas from one vessel to another, and show that it has been transferred.

5. Balance a beaker on a good-sized scales, and pour carbon dioxide into it.

Explain all that you have done, giving an account of the properties of carbon dioxide as you have observed them in the above experiments.

FIG. 25.

CARBONATES.

EXPERIMENT 77.

Apparatus for making carbon dioxide as in last experiment; caustic potash; any dilute acid; test-tube.

1. Pass carbon dioxide into a solution of caustic potash (potassium hydroxide or potassium hydrate) until it will absorb no more.

2. Add any dilute acid to some of the solution thus obtained.

What gas is given off when the acid is added?

How do you know?

Write the equations expressing the reactions which take place on passing the carbon dioxide into the caustic potash solution, and on adding an acid to the solution.

CARBONATES.

EXPERIMENT 78.

Apparatus for carbon dioxide ; lime-water ; filter ; dilute acid.

1. Pass carbon dioxide into 50 to 100 cubic centimeters of clear lime-water.
2. Filter off the white insoluble substance.
3. Try the action of a little dilute acid on it.

What evidence have you that it is calcium carbonate?

How could you easily distinguish between lime-water and a solution of caustic potash?

EXPERIMENT 79.

Apparatus for carbon dioxide ; lime-water.

1. Pass carbon dioxide first through a little water to wash it, and then into 50 to 100 cubic centimeters of clear lime-water.
2. After the solution has become clear, heat it.

What has taken place?

CARBON MONOXIDE.

EXPERIMENT 80.

Flask of about 4 oz. capacity; crystallized oxalic acid; concentrated sulphuric acid; two Woulff's flasks; solution of caustic soda; cylinders or bottles for collecting gas.

Put 10 grams crystallized oxalic acid and 50 to 60 grams concentrated sulphuric acid in an appropriate-sized flask. Connect with two Woulff's flasks containing caustic-soda solution. Heat the contents of the flask gently. Collect some of the gas over water. Set fire to the same, and notice the characteristic blue flame.

What is formed when the gas burns?

Why is the gas first passed through caustic soda?

EXPERIMENT 81.

Granulated copper oxide; hard-glass tube; apparatus for making carbon monoxide as used in last experiment; lime-water.

Put a gram or two of copper oxide in a hard-glass tube. Pass carbon monoxide through the tube and over the copper oxide, while gently heating the tube.

What change do you observe in the appearance of the copper oxide?

What happens when the gas is passed into lime-water after it has passed over the heated copper oxide? Why?

Express the chemical change by means of an equation.

FLAMES.

EXPERIMENT 82.*

Wire gauze; Bunsen burner.

1. Light a Bunsen burner. Bring down upon the flame a piece of brass or iron-wire gauze.

Does the flame pass through the gauze?

2. Apply a light above the gauze and above the outlet of the burner.

Is there any gas unburned above the gauze?

Why does the flame not pass through the gauze?

3. Turn on a Bunsen burner. Do not light the gas. Hold a piece of wire gauze about one and a half to two inches above the outlet. Apply a lighted match above the gauze.

Where is the flame?

What is below the gauze?

Prove it.

What is the principle upon which the miner's safety-lamp is constructed?

For what is it used?

---

* This experiment cannot be performed if spirit-lamps are used instead of gas-burners.

BROMINE AND HYDROBROMIC ACID.

EXPERIMENT 83.

Test-tube; potassium bromide; manganese dioxide; dilute sulphuric acid.

Mix together about a gram of potassium bromide and two grams of maganese dioxide. Pour upon the mixture, in a good-sized test-tube, sufficient dilute sulphuric acid to cover it. Heat gently.

What do you observe?

Perform this experiment where there is a good draught.

EXPERIMENT 84.

Test-tube; potassium bromide; concentrated sulphuric acid; potassium or sodium chloride.

1. In a test-tube put two or three small crystals of potassium bromide. Pour on them a few drops of concentrated sulphuric acid.

What do you see?

2. Treat two or three crystals of potassium or sodium chloride in the same way.

What difference is there between the two cases?

Explain the difference.

IODINE AND HYDRIODIC ACID.

EXPERIMENT 85.

Test-tube ; potassium iodide ; manganese dioxide ; concentrated sulphuric acid.

Mix about 1 gram potassium iodide with about twice its weight of manganese dioxide. Treat with 2–3 cubic centimeters of concentrated sulphuric acid in a test-tube. Heat gently.

What takes place ? Explain.

EXPERIMENT 86.

Iodine ; alcohol ; potassium iodide ; test-tubes.

Make solutions of iodine in water, in alcohol, and in a water solution of potassium iodide. In each case use one or two small crystals of iodine and a small test-tube. For the solution of potassium iodide dissolve a piece the size of a pea in two or three cubic centimeters of water.

Is iodine soluble in water?
Is it soluble in alcohol?
Is it soluble in a solution of potassium iodide?

IODINE AND HYDRIODIC ACID.

EXPERIMENT 87.

Starch ; iodine ; potassium iodide ; chlorine-water, made by passing chlorine gas into water.

1. Make some starch-paste by covering a few grains of starch in a porcelain evaporating-dish with cold water, grinding this to a paste, and pouring 200–300 cubic centimeters of boiling water on it.

2. After cooling add a few drops of this paste to a dilute water solution of iodine.

What change takes place ?

3. Now add a little of the paste to a dilute water solution of potassium iodide, prepared as in Exp. 86.

Is there any change of color ?

4. Add a drop or two of a solution of chlorine in water.

What takes place ?

Explain what you have seen.

Does chlorine alone form a blue compound with starch ?

EXPERIMENT 88.

Potassium iodide ; concentrated sulphuric acid.

Treat a few small crystals of potassium iodide with concentrated sulphuric acid.

What do you notice ?

Compare with the results obtained when potassium bromide and sodium chloride are used.

HYDROFLUORIC ACID.

EXPERIMENT 89.

Lead or platinum crucible; powdered fluor spar; concentrated sulphuric acid; wax or paraffin.

In a lead or platinum vessel put a few grams (5-6) of powdered fluor spar, and pour on it enough concentrated sulphuric acid to make a thick paste. Cover the surface of a piece of glass with a thin layer of wax or paraffin, and through this scratch some letters or figures, so as to leave the glass exposed where the scratches are made. Put the glass with the waxed side downward over the vessel containing the fluor spar, and let it stand for some hours. Then take off the glass and scrape off the coating.

What chemical changes have taken place in this experiment?

What is the change in the glass called?

Suppose marks had been made on the glass by a diamond, would the change be chemical or physical?

SULPHUR.

EXPERIMENT 90.

Small retort; roll sulphur.

Distil about 10 grams of roll sulphur from a small glass retort. Do not connect with a condenser.

Notice the changes.

Collect the liquid sulphur which distils over in a beaker containing cold water. What are its properties?

EXPERIMENT 91.

Roll sulphur; sand crucible.

In a covered sand or Hessian crucible melt about 20 grams of roll sulphur. Let it cool slowly, and when a thin crust has formed on the surface make a hole through this and pour out the sulphur. The inside of the crucible will be found lined with honey-yellow needles.

Take out a few crystals and examine them. Are they brittle or elastic?

What is their color?

Are they opaque, translucent, or transparent?

What changes take place in the crystals when the crucible is laid aside a few days?

SULPHUR.

EXPERIMENT 92.

Roll sulphur; carbon bisulphide.

Dissolve 2 to 3 grams roll sulphur in 5 to 10 cubic centimeters of carbon bisulphide. Put the solution in a small beaker, and allow the carbon bisulphide to evaporate by standing in the air.

What is the appearance of the crystals?
Are they dark yellow or bright yellow?
Are they brittle or elastic?
State in tabular form the properties of the two allotropic forms of sulphur.
What is allotropy?

EXPERIMENT 93.

Wide test-tube; sulphur; copper-foil.

In a wide test-tube heat 2–3 grams of sulphur to boiling. Introduce into it small pieces of copper-foil or sheet-copper. Or hold a narrow piece of sheet-copper so that the end just dips into the boiling sulphur.

What evidence have you that action takes place?
Compare the chemical action in this case with that which takes place when copper-foil is put into chlorine.

HYDROGEN SULPHIDE (SULPHURETTED HYDROGEN).

EXPERIMENT 94.

Apparatus as shown in Fig. 26; iron sulphide; dilute sulphuric acid; cylinders or bottles.

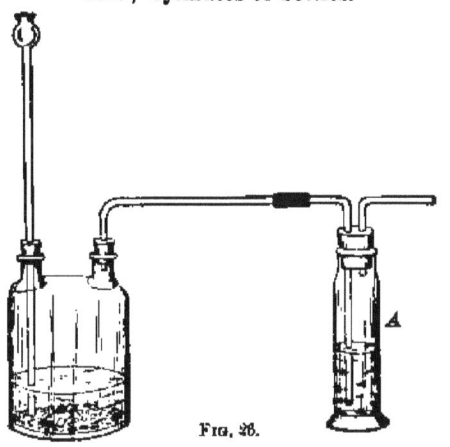

FIG. 26.

Arrange an apparatus as shown in Fig. 26. Put a small handful of sulphide of iron, FeS, in the flask, and pour cold, *dilute* sulphuric acid upon it.

1. Pass the gas through a little water contained in the wash-cylinder *A*. Pass some of the gas into water.

Is the gas soluble in water?

2. Collect some of the gas by displacement of air as in the case of chlorine and hydrochloric acid. It is heavier than air.

3. Set fire to some of the gas contained in a cylinder.

What products are formed?

Hydrochloric acid, water, ammonia, marsh gas, and hydrogen sulphide are all compounds of hydrogen. Compare them with special reference to their conduct towards oxygen.

HYDROGEN SULPHIDE.

EXPERIMENT 95.

Lead nitrate; zinc sulphate; arsenic trioxide (white arsenic); test-tubes; dilute hydrochloric acid; apparatus for making hydrogen sulphide as in last experiment.

Prepare a solution of lead nitrate by dissolving about a gram in 8–10 cubic centimeters of water in a test-tube; a solution of zinc sulphate of the same strength; and a solution of arsenic chloride by boiling about a gram of arsenic trioxide (white arsenic or arsenious acid) with 8–10 cubic centimeters of dilute hydrochloric acid in a test-tube. Pass hydrogen sulphide through each solution.

What do you observe in each case?

SULPHUR DIOXIDE.

EXERIMENT 96.

Solution of acid sodium sulphite; dropping-funnel; flask of 500 c.c. capacity; concentrated sulphuric acid; cylinder or bottle.

1. Arrange an apparatus as shown in Fig. 27. *A* is a funnel-tube provided with a stop-cock. In the flask put a 40 per cent solution of acid sodium sulphite; in the funnel, after closing the stop-cock, put ordinary concentrated sulphuric acid. Open the stop-cock slightly so that the acid *drops* into the solution below.

2. Pass some of the gas into a bottle containing water.

Is it soluble in water?

FIG. 27.

3. Fill a vessel by displacement of air. (It is more than twice as heavy as air.)

4. See whether the gas will burn or support combustion.

Is the gas colored? Is it transparent? Has it any odor? Does it burn?

In what experiment already performed was this gas formed?

EXPERIMENT 97.

Sulphur; porcelain crucible; bell-jar or wide-mouthed bottle; tripod; colored flowers.

Burn a gram or two of sulphur in a porcelain crucible under a bell-jar. Place over the crucible on a tripod some flowers.

What change takes place in the flowers?

Compare the action with the action of chlorine.

Does sulphur dioxide act in the same way that chlorine does?

SULPHURIC ACID.

EXPERIMENT 97a.

Table-syrup; evaporating-dish; concentrated sulphuric acid; test-tube.

In an evaporating-dish mix 8–10 cubic centimeters of ordinary table-syrup and the same quantity of concentrated sulphuric acid.

The sugar which is in solution in the syrup contains carbon, hydrogen, and oxygen. If the sulphuric acid should combine with the hydrogen and oxygen, what would be left?

What is the appearance of the substance which is left?

EXPERIMENT 97b.

Dilute sulphuric acid; barium chloride solution.

To 8–10 cubic centimeters of water in a test-tube add 4–5 drops of dilute sulphuric acid, and then add a few drops of a dilute solution of barium chloride, $BaCl_2$.*

Sulphuric acid can be detected by means of this reaction. The insoluble salt formed is barium sulphate, $BaSO_4$:

$$[H_2SO_4 + BaCl_2 = BaSO_4 + 2HCl.]$$

---

*When the expression "dilute solution" is used it generally means a solution containing 1 part of the salt in 10–15 parts of water.

PHOSPHORUS.

EXPERIMENT 98.

Porcelain crucible or evaporating-dish; phosphorus; iodine.

Bring together in a porcelain crucible or evaporating-dish a piece of phosphorus about the size of a pea and about the same quantity of iodine.

What takes place?

What is the cause of the light and heat?

Compare the action of phosphorus towards iodine with its action towards oxygen.

What other examples have you had of the direct combination of two elements by simple contact?

What examples have you had of direct combination of two elements at elevated temperature?

EXPERIMENT 98a.

Disodium phosphate; ammonium chloride; ammonia; magnesium sulphate; test-tube.

To 8-10 cubic centimeters of water in a test-tube add 4-5 drops of a dilute solution of disodium phosphate, and then add 4-5 drops of a dilute solution of each of the substances ammonium chloride, ammonia, and magnesium sulphate, $MgSO_4$.

Phosphoric acid can be detected by means of this reaction. The insoluble salt formed is ammonium magnesium phosphate, NH_4MgPO_4:

$$[HNa_2PO_4 + MgSO_4 + NH_3 = NH_4MgPO_4 + Na_2SO_4.]$$

ARSENIC.

EXPERIMENT 99.

Apparatus as shown in Fig. 28; granulated zinc; dilute sulphuric acid; granulated calcium chloride; solution of arsenic chloride.

Arrange an apparatus as shown in Fig. 28. The first horizontal tube should contain granulated calcium chloride for the purpose of drying the gases. The burner is not to be lighted in this experiment (see next exp.). Put 10–15 grams granulated zinc in the

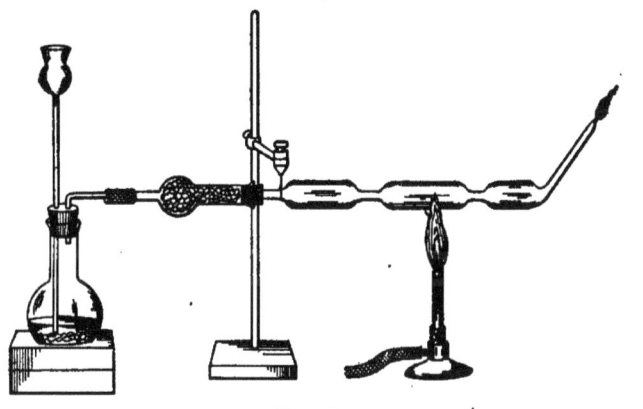

FIG. 28.

flask and pour 20–30 cubic centimeters of dilute sulphuric acid on it. When the air is all out of the vessel and the hydrogen is lighted, slowly add 5–10 drops of a solution of arsenic chloride prepared by dissolving arsenic trioxide, As_2O_3, in dilute hydrochloric acid, as in Exp. 95.

What change takes place in the flame?
Is the color changed?
Are fumes given off? (See Exp. 100.)

$As_2O_3 + 6HCl = 2AsCl_3 + 3H_2O$

$Zn + H_2SO_4 = ZnSO_4 + 2H$

$6H + AsCl_3 = AsH_3 + 3HCl$

$CaCl_2 + H_2O =$

$2AsH_3 + 6O = As_2O_3 + 3H_2O$

$2AsH_3 + 3O = 2As + 3H_2O$

$AsH_3 = As + 3H$

ARSENIC.

EXPERIMENT 100.

Apparatus used in last experiment; piece of white porcelain.

1. Into the flame of the burning hydrogen and arsine produced in the last experiment introduce a piece of porcelain, as the bottom of a small porcelain dish or crucible, or a bit of a broken plate, and notice the appearance of the spots.

2. Heat by means of a Bunsen burner the tube through which the gas is passing, which should be of hard glass.

Explain what you have seen.

EXPERIMENT 101.

Arsenic trioxide; finely-powdered charcoal; ignition-tube.

Mix together about equal small quantities of arsenic oxide and finely-powdered charcoal. Heat the mixture in a small dry tube of hard glass, closed at one end.

What change takes place?

What is this kind of action called?

What do you notice that reminds you of the preceding experiment?

ANTIMONY.

EXPERIMENT 102.

Apparatus as shown in Fig. 28; tartar emetic; piece of white porcelain.

Make some stibine, using the same kind of apparatus as that for making arsine. Instead of a solution of arsenic use a solution of tartar emetic, which contains antimony.

What differences, if any, do you notice between what takes place in this case and what you saw in Experiment 99?

EXPERIMENT 103.

Same apparatus as in preceding experiment; piece of white porcelain.

Introduce a piece of porcelain in the flame and notice the deposit or antimony spot.

Compare the spots with those formed with arsenic.

Is there any difference in the appearance?

Heat the porcelain on which the spots are and notice whether any change takes place.

POTASSIUM.

EXPERIMENT 104.

Wood-ashes; filter; red litmus-paper; potassium carbonate; evaporating-dish; water-bath; test-tube; dilute hydrochloric acid.

1. Treat about a pound of wood-ashes with water. Filter off the solution, and examine it by means of red litmus-paper.

Is the solution alkaline?

2. Examine some potassium carbonate.

Does its solution act in the same way?

3. Evaporate to dryness the solution obtained from the wood-ashes. Collect the dry residue and treat it in a test-tube with a little dilute hydrochloric acid.

Is a gas given off?

What is it?

EXPERIMENT 105.*

Potassium; red litmus-paper.

Throw a small piece of potassium not larger than a pea upon water.

What takes place?

What is the color of the flame?

What difference is there between the action of sodium and of potassium on water?

Is the solution after the action alkaline?

Why?

---

* See caution, Experiment 85.

POTASSIUM.

EXPERIMENT 106.

Crystallized potassium iodide; iodine; test-tubes; concentrated sulphuric acid.

1. Examine a bottle of crystallized potassium iodide. Taste a little. Dissolve one or two of the crystals in water.

2. Add one or two crystals of iodine to the solution. Does the iodine dissolve?

3. Heat one or two of the crystals.

Does the substance contain water of crystallization?

4. Treat a crystal or two with a few drops of concentrated sulphuric acid in a test-tube.

What takes place?

To what is the appearance of violet vapors due? See Experiment 88.

EXPERIMENT 106a.

Potassium carbonate; iron sauce-pan; quicklime; stout iron wire; glass siphon.

1. Dissolve 25 grams potassium carbonate in 250–300 cubic centimeters of water. Heat to boiling in an iron (or silver) vessel, and gradually add slaked lime made from 12–15 grams good quicklime. During the operation the mass should be stirred with a stout iron wire.

2. After the solution is cool, draw it off by means of a glass siphon into a bottle. This may be used in experiments in which caustic potash is required.

Explain what has taken place.

Write the equation expressing the chemical change.

What is left in the iron vessel?

POTASSIUM.

EXPERIMENT 107.

Potassium nitrate; powdered charcoal.

Mix together 15 grams finely powdered potassium nitrate and 2.5 grams powdered charcoal. Set fire to the mass.

What is left?
What was given off?
What is gunpowder made of?
What is the cause of its explosive power?

AMMONIUM SALTS.

EXPERIMENT 108.

Concentrated hydrochloric acid; concentrated ammonia; concentrated nitric acid; sulphuric acid.

1. Place near each other two vessels, one containing about 10 cubic centimeters of strong hydrochloric acid, and the other about 10 cubic centimeters of strong ammonia.

Explain what you see.

2. Try the same experiment using nitric acid instead of hydrochloric acid.

What takes place?

3. Finally, try the experiment using sulphuric acid and ammonia.

What difference is there between this case and the other two?

How do you explain this?

AMMONIUM SALTS.

EXPERIMENT 109.

Piece of platinum foil or of porcelain; ammonium chloride.

On a piece of platinum-foil or porcelain heat a little ammonium chloride.

What is the result?

What is the difference between this process and the process which we call boiling?

What would happen if a piece of ice were heated to the temperature of boiling water?

FLAME REACTIONS.

EXPERIMENT 110.

Platinum wire; sodium carbonate; potassium carbonate; piece of blue glass.

1. Prepare some pieces of platinum wire, 8 to 10 cm. long, with a small loop on the end. After thoroughly cleaning them, insert one into sodium carbonate, withdraw it and then notice the color it gives to the flame.

2. Try another with potassium carbonate.

3. Try a mixture of potassium carbonate and sodium carbonate.

What is the color of the flame?

Could you tell that potassium is in the mixture by looking at the flame with the naked eye?

4. Look through blue glass at the flame caused by potassium alone; at that caused by sodium alone; and at that caused by potassium and sodium.

Can you tell whether potassium is present or not when you use the blue glass?

POTASSIUM, SODIUM, AMMONIUM.

EXPERIMENT 110a.

Potassium chloride; sodium chloride; ammonium chloride; chlorplatinic acid (platinum chloride).

1. To 4–5 cubic centimeters of a dilute solution of potassium chloride add 5–10 drops of chlorplatinic acid ("platinum chloride"), H_2PtCl_6.

Potassium can be detected by means of this reaction. The difficultly soluble salt formed is potassium chlorplatinate, K_2PtCl_6.

2. See whether platinum chloride gives a precipitate with a solution of a sodium salt.

How could you distinguish between a sodium and a potassium salt?

3. Add to 4–5 cubic centimeters of ammonium chloride solution 2–3 drops of chlorplatinic acid.

The precipitate formed is ammonium chlorplatinate, $(NH_4)_2PtCl_6$.

How could you distinguish between potassium and sodium? between potassium and ammonium?

CALCIUM.

EXPERIMENT 111.

Limestone or marble; ordinary hydrochloric acid; evaporating-dish; water-bath; sulphuric acid.

1. Dissolve 10 to 20 grams of limestone or marble in ordinary hydrochloric acid. Evaporate to dryness. Expose a few pieces of the residue to the air.

Does it become moist?

In what experiments has calcium chloride been used, and for what purposes?

What would happen if sulphuric acid were added to calcium chloride?

2. Try it.

Explain what takes place.

Is the residue soluble or insoluble in water?

How could you tell whether a given substance is calcium chloride, sodium chloride, potassium chloride, or ammonium chloride?

3. Try the experiment with substances the composition of which is unknown to you.

What happens when a solution of ammonium carbonate is added to a solution of a calcium salt?

Explain the reaction.

CALCIUM.

EXPERIMENT 112.

Quicklime.

1. To 40 or 50 grams good quicklime add 100 cubic centimeters of water.

What takes place?

2. Afterwards dilute to 2 to 3 liters and put the whole in a well-stoppered bottle. The undissolved lime will settle to the bottom, and in the course of some hours the solution above will become clear. Carefully pour off some of the clear solution.

What takes place when some of the solution is exposed to the air?

When the gases from the lungs are passed through it?

When carbon dioxide is passed through it?

What takes place when dilute sulphuric acid is added to lime-water?

Is calcium sulphate difficultly or easily soluble in water?

Has lime-water an alkaline reaction?

What reaction would you expect to take place between lime and nitric acid?

CALCIUM.

EXPERIMENT 113.

Gypsum; porcelain crucible.

1. Heat some powdered gypsum in a porcelain crucible, using as small a flame as will cause water to be given off; or heat in an air-bath to about 180°.

2. Examine what is left and see whether it will become solid when mixed with a little water so as to form a paste.

3. See whether gypsum itself will act in the same way with water.

Explain what you have done.

EXPERIMENT 113a.

Gypsum; barium chloride.

1. Make a solution of calcium sulphate by letting about 50 cubic centimeters of water stand in contact with 3–4 grams of powdered gypsum.

The presence of a sulphate in solution can be detected by the same reaction as that used in the case of sulphuric acid. See Experiment 97b.

What is this reaction?

2. See whether calcium sulphate is in the solution just prepared.

COPPER.

EXPERIMENT 115.

Copper sulphate; strip of zinc; strip of sheet iron.

1. Into a solution of 1 or 2 grams of copper sulphate in 15–20 cubic centimeters of water insert a strip of zinc.

Explain what takes place.

Compare the action with that which takes place when zinc acts upon sulphuric acid.

2. Perform a similar experiment, using a strip of sheet-iron instead of zinc.

Compare this with the previous experiment.

EXPERIMENT 116.

Copper sulphate; caustic soda or potash.*

1. Add some caustic soda or potash to a small quantity of a cold solution of copper sulphate in a test-tube.

What do you notice?

2. After noticing the appearance of the precipitate first formed, heat.

What change takes place?

Explain this.

Express the chemical change by the proper equation.

---

* For test-tube experiments use a solution containing about 10 grams of either caustic soda or potash in 100 cubic centimeters of water. The solution of copper sulphate is prepared by adding 5–10 drops of such a solution as that used in Exp. 115 to 8–10 cubic centimeters of water.

COPPER.

EXPERIMENT 116a.

Copper sulphate; hydrochloric acid; hydrogen sulphide; dilute nitric acid; ammonia.

1. Prepare a dilute solution of copper sulphate (see note to Exp. 116), and add to it 5-10 drops of dilute hydrochloric acid.

2. Pass hydrogen sulphide through this solution for some time.

The insoluble substance formed is copper sulphide, CuS.

3. Filter and wash. Treat with 5-10 cubic centimeters of dilute nitric acid, and then add 5-10 cubic centimeters of water. What is in the solution thus formed?

4. Add ammonia to 1-2 cubic centimeters of this solution. How could you detect copper?

SILVER.

EXPERIMENT 117.

Silver coin; dilute nitric acid; common salt; filter; porcelain crucible; small piece of sheet zinc; dilute sulphuric acid; evaporating-dish; water-bath; bottle wrapped in dark paper.

1. Dissolve a ten or twenty-five cent piece in dilute nitric acid.

What action takes place?

2. Dilute the solution to 200 to 300 cubic centimeters with water.

What is the color of the solution?

What does this indicate?

Does this color prove that copper is present?

3. Add a solution of common salt (prepared by adding 100 cubic centimeters of water to 15–20 grams of salt and filtering after the salt has dissolved) until it ceases to produce a precipitate.

What change takes place?

4. Filter off the white silver chloride and carefully wash with hot water.

5. Dry the precipitate on the filter, by putting the funnel with the filter and precipitate in a warm place, or in an air-bath heated to 110°.

6. Remove the precipitate from the filter and put it into a porcelain crucible. Heat gently with a small flame until the chloride is melted.

7. Cut out a piece of sheet-zinc large enough to cover the silver chloride. Lay it on the silver chloride. Now add 15–20 drops of water and 4–5 drops of dilute sulphuric acid, and let the whole stand for twenty-four hours.

What takes place?

8. Take out the piece of zinc and wash the silver with a little dilute sulphuric acid, and then with water.

9. Dissolve the silver in dilute nitric acid and evaporate to dryness on the water-bath, so that the excess of nitric acid is driven off. Dissolve the residue in water, and put the solution either in a bottle of dark glass or one wrapped in dark paper.

SILVER.

EXPERIMENT 118.

Solution of silver nitrate prepared in last experiment; test-tubes; sodium chloride; potassium bromide; potassium iodide; ammonia.

1. To 8–10 cubic centimeters of water in a test-tube add 5 to 10 drops of the solution of silver nitrate just prepared.

2. To this dilute solution add a few drops of a solution of sodium chloride.

What takes place?

3. Place it aside where the light can shine upon it, and notice the change of color which gradually takes place.

4. In the same way make the bromide by adding potassium bromide, and the iodide by adding potassium iodide to silver nitrate.

What extensive practical use is made of the change produced in silver salts by light?

5. Try the effect of adding a few drops of a solution of ammonia to each of the test-tubes used in 4.

What differences do you notice?

Given hydrochloric acid or common salt, how could you distinguish between a silver salt and a copper salt?

IRON.

EXPERIMENT 119.

Iron wire; dilute hydrochloric acid; solution of sodium hydroxide; concentrated nitric acid.

1. Dissolve three or four pieces of iron wire, each an inch or two long, in 8–10 cubic centimeters of dilute hydrochloric acid in a test-tube.

What is given off? The odor is caused by other gases formed from impurities in the iron.

What remains undissolved?

What is in solution?

Write the equation representing the action of the acid on the iron.

2. To four or five drops of the solution in 8–10 cubic centimeters of water in a test-tube add at once as many drops of a dilute solution of sodium hydroxide.

What is the chemical change?

Write the equation.

3. Let the tube with its contents stand open, and shake it up from time to time.

What changes do you notice?

Explain what you have seen.

4. Prepare a dilute solution of ferrous chloride as in 2, and heat to boiling; then add a few drops of concentrated nitric acid, and boil again. Repeat this two or three times.

What change in color takes place?

What is now in solution?

5. Add four or five drops of sodium hydroxide to the solution.

What is the chemical change?

EXPERIMENT 119—(*Continued*).

Compare the precipitate with that in the tube which you have put aside (see 3).

6. Add a little zinc and hydrochloric acid to the solution of ferric chloride, and let stand until the reddish-yellow color disappears.

In what way has the ferric chloride been affected? Explain.

Add a little sodium hydroxide to some of the solution.

What is formed?

CHROMIUM.

EXPERIMENT 120.

Potassium bichromate; potassium hydroxide; evaporating-dish; water-bath.

To a solution of 10 to 20 grams potassium bichromate slowly add a solution of potassium hydroxide * until the color has turned pure yellow. Evaporate to crystallization.

What is the product? Compare it with potassium bichromate.

Explain the change.

EXPERIMENT 121.

Potassium chromate; dilute nitric acid; evaporating-dish; water-bath.

To the solution of the yellow salt just obtained add dilute nitric acid until the color has turned red. Evaporate to crystallization.

What is the product?

Explain the change.

EXPERIMENT 122.

Potassium chromate; potassium bichromate; hydrochloric acid; test-tubes.

Treat a gram of potassium chromate and a gram of potassium bichromate separately in test-tubes with hydrochloric acid.

Explain what takes place.

---

* Prepared as recommended in foot note to Exp. 116.

CHROMIUM.

EXPERIMENT 123.

Potassium chromate or bichromate ; barium chloride ; lead acetate or nitrate.

Add a little of a solution* of potassium chromate or bichromate to a solution of barium chloride, and to a solution of lead acetate or nitrate.

EXPERIMENT 123a.

Barium chloride ; lead acetate or nitrate ; sodium or potassium sulphate.

Add a little of a solution of potassium or sodium sulphate to a solution of barium chloride, and to a solution of lead acetate or nitrate.

How do the results compare with those obtained with the chromate?

Compare the composition of potassium chromate with that of potassium sulphate.

What resemblance is there?

---

* The solutions here referred to are prepared by dissolving 1 part of each salt in 10–15 parts of water. Of such solutions use only 5–10 drops in 8–10 cubic centimeters of water in a test-tube.

EXPERIMENT 123b.

Potassium bichromate; dilute hydrochloric acid; alcohol; ammonia; ammonium sulphide; sodium hydroxide.

1. To 5–10 cubic centimeters of a solution of potassium bichromate (see note to Exp. 123) in a test-tube add 10–15 drops of hydrochloric acid and 10–15 drops of alcohol, and boil. What change takes place?

[Under the conditions the chromium is changed to chromic chloride, $CrCl_3$, and the potassium to potassium chloride, while some of the oxyen of the bichromate acts upon the alcohol, converting it into aldehyde:

$$K_2Cr_2O_7 + 8HCl = 2KCl + 2CrCl_3 + 4H_2O + 3O;$$
$$\underset{\text{Alcohol.}}{3C_2H_6O} + 3O = \underset{\text{Aldehyde.}}{3C_2H_4O} + 3H_2O.]$$

2. To 10–15 drops of the solution of chromic chloride obtained in 1 add 5–10 cubic centimeters of water, and then add a few drops of ammonia and of ammonium sulphide.*

Chromium does not form a sulphide, but, under the conditions named, the hydroxide, $Cr(OH)_3$, is precipitated.

3. To a little of the dilute solution of chromic chloride (same strength as in 2) in a test-tube add a few drops of a cold solution of sodium hydroxide.

The precipitate first formed is chromic hydroxide.

4. Add more of the solution of sodium hydroxide.

$$Cr(OH)_3 + NaOH = NaCrO_2 + 2H_2O.$$

The salt $NaCrO_2$ is soluble in water.

How could you detect chromium?

---

* To prepare ammonium sulphide pass hydrogen sulphide gas into 50–100 cubic centimeters of a water solution of ammonia, as obtained in Exp. 51, until the gas is no longer absorbed, and then add an equal volume of the same solution of ammonia. The solution has a disagreeable smell, and blackens the skin.

LEAD.

Experiment 124.*

Lead acetate; acetic acid; wide-mouthed bottle; strip sheet-zinc.

Dissolve 6 or 8 grams lead acetate (sugar of lead) in a liter of water, add a few drops of acetic acid, and put the solution in a wide-mouthed bottle. Suspend a piece of sheet-zinc in the middle of the solution, and let it stand for a day or two.

Describe what has taken place.

Compare with the action of zinc on copper sulphate.

Compare with the action of iron on sulphuric acid.

Give the equations expressing each of the reactions referred to.

---

* It will be best for the teacher to perform this experiment and then set the vessel aside. Sometimes the lead-tree formed is very beautiful.

LEAD.

Experiment 124a.

Sheet-lead; shallow dish or plate; hydrochloric acid; sulphuric acid; hydrogen sulphide; lead acetate; piece of iron; potassium ferrocyanide.

1. Cut a piece of sheet-lead an inch or two square and partly cover it with water in a shallow dish. Allow it to stand for several days, renewing the water from time to time. Then filter off and examine the water to see whether there is any lead in solution.

(*a*) To 8–10 cubic centimeters of the water in a test-tube add 2–3 drops of hydrochloric acid.

Is a precipitate formed?

(*b*) To another small portion of the water add a few drops of sulphuric acid.

Is a precipitate formed?

(*c*) Into a third portion pass a little hydrogen sulphide.

What takes place?

(*d*) Try the same experiments with a very dilute solution of lead acetate, prepared by dissolving a piece the size of a small pea in 8–10 cubic centimeters of water.

Of what practical importance is the above experiment?

2. Try the same experiment with a piece of iron.

Is there any iron in solution? [The easiest way to find this out is to add a few drops of a solution of potassium ferricyanide* or red prussiate of potash, when, if iron is in solution, a blue color will be seen.]

---

* See Experiment 9.

LEAD.

EXPERIMENT 125.

Minium or red lead; dilute nitric acid.

Treat a gram or two of minium with 8–10 cubic centimeters of ordinary dilute nitric acid in a test-tube, and note the change in color.

Does lead pass into solution?

How do you know?

EXPERIMENT 126.

Lead peroxide; dilute hydrochloric acid.

Treat a gram or two of lead peroxide with 8–10 cubic centimeters of dilute hydrochloric acid in a test-tube.

In what form is the lead after the experiment?

Is the product soluble or insoluble in water?

FERMENTATION.

EXPERIMENT 127.

Apparatus as shown in Fig. 29; commercial grape-sugar or table-syrup; fresh brewer's yeast; lime-water; potassium hydroxide.

Dissolve 150 grams commercial grape-sugar, or 150 cubic centimeters of table syrup, in 1 to 2 liters of water in a flask. Connect the flask by means of a bent glass tube with a cylinder or bottle containing clear lime-water. The vessel containing the lime-water must be

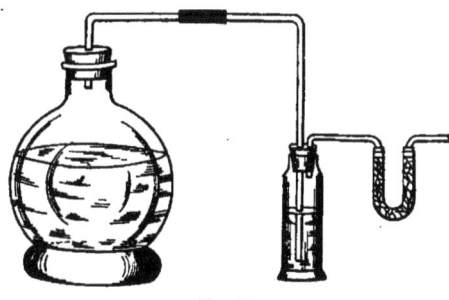

FIG. 29.

provided with a cork with two holes. Through one of these passes the tube from the fermentation-flask; through the other a tube connecting with a vessel containing solid caustic potash, the object of which is to prevent the carbon dioxide in the air from acting upon the lime-water. The arrangement of the apparatus is shown in Fig. 29. Now add to the solution of grape-sugar or syrup some fresh brewer's yeast; close the connections and allow to stand.

What changes take place?

Explain all you have seen.

SOAP.

EXPERIMENT 128.

Small iron pot; lard; sodium hydroxide; common salt.

1. In a small iron pot boil for an hour or two a quarter of a pound of lard with a solution of 40 grams caustic soda or sodium hydroxide in 250 cubic centimeters of water. After cooling add a concentrated solution of common salt.

Explain what takes place.
What is the product?

2. Dissolve some of the product in water.

HARD WATER.

EXPERIMENT 129.

Carbon dioxide generator; lime-water; solution of soap.

1. Make some hard water by passing carbon dioxide through 200–300 cubic centimeters of lime-water until the precipitate first formed has dissolved again. Filter.

2. Make a solution of soap by shaking up a few shavings of soap with water. Filter.

3. Add the solution of soap to the hard water.

Is a precipitate formed?

4. Rub a piece of soap between the hands wet with the hard water.

Explain what you observe.

EXPERIMENT 130.

Powdered gypsum; solution of soap made as in last experiment.

Make some hard water by shaking a liter or two of water with two or three grams of powdered gypsum. Perform with it the same experiments as those first performed with the water containing calcium carbonate.

TANNIC ACID.

EXPERIMENT 131.

Powdered nutgalls; ferrous sulphate.

1. Boil 10 grams of powdered nutgalls with 60 cubic centimeters of water, adding water from time to time. A solution of tannin is thus obtained. Filter after standing.

2. In a test-tube add to 8–10 cubic centimeters of this solution a few drops of a solution of copperas (ferrous sulphate).

What is formed?

PREPARATION OF SOLUTIONS.

For the work now to be done various solutions will be needed. The preparation of most of these has already been described. For the others observe the same general rules. In the case of a solid, dissolve 1 part in 10 parts water, and in working with this solution in test-tubes use only 5–10 drops diluted with 8–10 cubic centimeters of water. In some cases it may be necessary to use more concentrated solutions. Whenever a solution, for the preparation of which the general rules will not suffice, is referred to after this, the method of preparation will be described. Whenever the direction is given to "add a little," add a few drops of the dilute solution at first, and if, for any reason, it appears desirable to add more, do so, and note the effect.

CHLORIDES.

EXPERIMENT 132.

1. Determine which of the chlorides are insoluble or difficultly soluble in water.

This you can do by adding hydrochloric acid or a solution of some soluble chloride, as sodium chloride, to a solution of a soluble salt of the element you wish to experiment upon. Thus, for example, suppose you wish to know whether copper chloride is soluble or insoluble in water. You know that copper sulphate is soluble in water, as you have worked with its solution. If copper chloride is insoluble in water, then on adding hydrochloric acid or a solution of sodium chloride to the solution of copper sulphate, a *precipitate* of copper chloride will be formed.

2. In your experiments use salts of potassium, calcium, magnesium, zinc, copper, mercury (both mercuric and mercurous* salts), silver, aluminium, iron (both ferrous and ferric salts), manganese, chromium, lead, and tin. Which are the insoluble chlorides?

3. Try the action of sulphuric acid on several chlorides. What is given off? How do you know?

---

* A solution of mercurous nitrate, $HgNO_3$, is prepared by treating a small globule of mercury the size of a pea with 4–5 cubic centimeters of dilute nitric acid. The quantity of acid should not be sufficient to dissolve all the mercury. Dilute the solution thus obtained with 5–10 times its bulk of water.

NITRATES.

EXPERIMENT 133.

1. Determine whether any of the nitrates are insoluble or difficultly soluble in water.

Work in the same way as with the chlorides.

2. Try the action of sulphuric acid on several nitrates.

What is given off on gently warming the mixture?

How do you know?

3. Heat some nitrates to a high temperature in a crucible.

What takes place?

How could you distinguish between a chloride and a nitrate, if both were soluble?

SULPHATES.

EXPERIMENT 134.

1. Determine which of the sulphates are insoluble or difficultly soluble in water.

Which are they?

2. Try the action of hydrochloric and of nitric acid on some sulphates.

Do you notice any change?

How could you distinguish between a chloride, a nitrate, and a sulphate?

See Experiments 97*b* and 113*a*.

CARBONATES.

EXPERIMENT 135.

1. Determine which of the carbonates are insoluble or difficultly soluble in water. After having obtained a precipitate, determine whether it is a carbonate or not by filtering, and treating the washed precipitate with hydrochloric acid.

Which carbonates are difficultly soluble or insoluble in water?

Which salts give, with a soluble carbonate, precipitates which are not carbonates?

2. Try the action of hydrochloric, of nitric, and of sulphuric acid on several carbonates.

What is given off?

How do you know?

SULPHIDES.

EXPERIMENT 136.

1. Determine with which metals hydrogen sulphide forms insoluble sulphides, by making solutions containing salts of the different metals, and passing hydrogen sulphide through them successively.

Which are the insoluble sulphides?

2. Prepare solutions of salts of the same metals used in 1, and add a little hydrochloric acid to each. Then pass hydrogen sulphide through those solutions with which hydrochloric acid does not give precipitates.

With which ones does hydrogen sulphide give precipitates?

3. To those solutions with which hydrogen sulphide does not give precipitates add ammonium sulphide.

Which solutions give precipitates with ammonium sulphide?

HOW TO ANALYZE SUBSTANCES.

In order to analyze substances chemists make use of reactions like those you have studied in Experiments 132, 133, 134, 135, and 136. To learn to analyze complicated substances, long practice and careful study of a great many facts are necessary. But simple substances can be analyzed by the aid of such facts as you have already learned. You have learned, for example, that certain chlorides are insoluble in water; that certain sulphides are insoluble in dilute hydrochloric acid; and that other sulphides which are soluble in dilute hydrochloric acid are insoluble in neutral or alkaline solutions. Advantage is taken of these and other similar facts to classify substances according to their reactions. A convenient classification for purposes of analysis is the following:

GROUP I. Metals whose chlorides are insoluble or difficultly soluble in water. This group includes: *Silver*, *lead*, and *mercury* in mercurous salts.

GROUP II. Metals not included in Group I, whose sulphides are insoluble in dilute hydrochloric or nitric acid. This group includes: *Copper*, *mercury* (as mercuric salt), *bismuth*, *antimony*, *arsenic*, and *tin*.

GROUP III. Metals not included in Groups I and II, whose sulphides are precipitated by ammonium sulphide and ammonia. This group includes: *Aluminium, chromium, nickel, cobalt, iron, zinc,* and *manganese.*

GROUP IV. Metals not included in Groups I, II, and III, which are precipitated by ammonium carbonate, ammonia, and ammonium chloride. This group includes: *Barium, strontium,* and *calcium.*

GROUP V. Metals not included in Groups I, II, III, and IV, which are precipitated by disodium phosphate, HNa_2PO_4, ammonia, and ammonium chloride. This group includes: *Magnesium.*

GROUP VI. Metals not included in Groups I, II, III, IV, and V. This group includes: *Sodium, potassium,* and *ammonium.*

1. Now, suppose you have a substance given you for analysis. The first thing to do is to get the substance in solution. See whether it dissolves in water. If it does not, try dilute hydrochloric acid. If it does not dissolve in hydrochloric acid, try nitric acid; and if it does not dissolve in nitric acid, try a mixture of nitric and hydrochloric acids. If concentrated acid is used, evaporate to dryness on a water-bath before proceeding further. Then dissolve in water, and add a few drops of hydrochloric acid. If a precipitate is formed, continue to add the acid drop by drop until a precipitate is no longer formed. Filter and wash.

What may this precipitate contain?

2. Pass hydrogen sulphide through the filtrate for some time and let stand. Filter and wash.

If a precipitate is formed, what may it contain?

3. Add ammonia and ammonium sulphide to the filtrate. Filter and wash.

If a precipitate is formed, what may it contain?

4. Add ammonium carbonate, ammonia, and ammonium chloride to the filtrate. Filter and wash.

If a precipitate is formed, what may it contain?

5. Add disodium phosphate, ammonia, and ammonium chloride to the filtrate. Filter and wash.

If a precipitate is formed, what may it contain?

What may be in the filtrate?

EXAMPLES FOR PRACTICE.

Before attempting anything in the way of systematic analysis it will be well to experiment in a more general way, with the object of determining which one of a given list of substances a certain specimen is.

The list below contains the names of the principal substances with which you have thus far had to deal in your work. You have handled them and have seen how they act toward different substances. Suppose now that a substance is given you, and you know simply that it is one of those named in the list, how would you go to work to find out which one it is? You have a right to judge by anything in the appearance or in the conduct of the substance. If you reach a conclusion, see whether you are right by further experiments. After your work is finished write out a clear account of what you have done, and state clearly your reasons for the conclusion which you have reached.

For example, suppose sodium chloride is given you. You see it is a white solid. On heating it in a small tube you see that it does not melt, but it breaks up into smaller pieces with a crackling sound. It is soluble in water. Hydrochloric acid causes no change when added to a little of the solid. Is it a carbonate? Sulphuric acid causes evolution of a gas. Has this an odor? How does it appear when allowed to escape into the air? Is it nitric acid? Collect some of it in water. How does this solution act on a solution of silver nitrate? By this time you have evidence that you are dealing with a chloride, but you do not yet know which chloride it is. It cannot be ammonium chloride. Why? It may be either potassium or sodium chloride. Moisten a clean platinum wire with distilled water, dip it into the powdered substance, and heat in a flame. What color?* You now have good reasons for believing that the substance you are dealing with is sodium chloride. To convince yourself, get a small piece of sodium chloride from the bottle known to contain it, and make a series of parallel experiments with this and see whether you get exactly the same results that you got with the specimen you were examining. If not, account for the differences.

By careful work there will be no serious difficulty in determining which one of the substances in the list you are dealing with.

---

* In making the color-test, always examine the flame through a piece of blue glass before deciding that the substance is a sodium salt. The color of the potassium flame is readily obscured by traces of sodium salts which may be present as impurities. (See Exp. 110, 4.)

LIST OF SUBSTANCES FOR EXAMINATION.

1. Sugar.
2. Mercuric oxide.
3. Calc-spar.
4. Marble.
5. Copper.
6. Hydrochloric acid.
7. Nitric acid.
8. Sulphuric acid.
9. Zinc.
10. Tin.
11. Tartaric acid.
12. Sodium carbonate.
13. Ferrous sulphate (Copperas).
14. Roll-sulphur.
15. Iron-filings.
16. Carbon bisulphide.
17. Lead.
18. Potassium chlorate.
19. Manganese dioxide.
20. Charcoal.
21. Calcium sulphate (Gypsum).
22. Copper oxide.
23. Ammonium chloride.
24. Calcium oxide (Quicklime).
25. Sodium nitrate.
26. Ammonium nitrate.
27. Sodium chloride.
28. Potassium bromide.
29. Potassium iodide.
30. Iron sulphide.
31. Potassium carbonate.
32. Potassium nitrate.
33. Potassium bichromate.
34. Red lead (Minium).
35. Lead carbonate.

[The teacher will, of course, select the substance and give it to the pupil without any suggestion as to what it is. After the pupil has shown that he can tell with certainty which substance he has, some simple mixtures of substances selected from the above list may next be given for examination. Thus charcoal and copper oxide; zinc and tin; mercuric oxide and iron filings; etc., etc.]

EXPERIMENT 137.

1. Prepare dilute solutions of silver nitrate, $AgNO_3$, lead nitrate, $Pb(NO_3)_2$, and mercurous nitrate, $HgNO_3$.

2. Add to a small quantity of each separately in test-tubes a little hydrochloric acid.

What is formed?

3. Heat each tube with contents, and then let cool.

What difference do you observe?

4. After cooling, add a little ammonia to the contents of each tube.

What takes place in each case?

How could you distinguish between silver, lead, and mercury?

5. Mix the solutions of silver nitrate, lead nitrate, and mercurous nitrate, and add a little of the mixture to considerable water in a test-tube. Add hydrochloric acid as long as it causes the formation of a precipitate. Heat to boiling. Filter rapidly and wash with hot water.

What is in the filtrate, and what is on the filter?

6. Let the filtrate cool.

What evidence have you that there is anything present in it?

7. Add sulphuric acid to a little of the filtrate.

8. Pass hydrogen sulphide through a little of the filtrate.

9. Pour ammonia on the filter, and wash out with water. Then *acidify* the filtrate with nitric acid.

What evidence do you get of the presence of silver and of mercury?

STUDY OF GROUP II.

EXPERIMENT 138.

1. Prepare dilute solutions of copper sulphate, mercuric chloride, arsenic chloride (see Exp. 95), and of tin chloride (made by dissolving tin in hydrochloric acid). [Bismuth and antimony are omitted, as their presence gives rise to difficulties hard to deal with intelligently at this stage.] Add a little hydrochloric acid to the solutions of copper sulphate and of mercuric chloride.

2. Pass hydrogen sulphide through a small quantity of each of the solutions.

What takes place? What are the substances formed?

3. Filter and wash. Treat each precipitate with a solution of ammonium sulphide.

What takes place? Add dilute sulphuric acid to the filtrates.

What takes place?

4. Treat the precipitates obtained from the copper and the mercury salts with warm concentrated nitric acid.

Does either one dissolve easily? What is the color of the solution?

5. Treat a little of the solution obtained in 4 with ammonia.

What is the result? How can you detect the presence of copper?

6. Treat with a mixture of nitric and hydrochloric acid the precipitate which is not readily dissolved by nitric acid alone. Evaporate the acid. Add water, and then a solution of tin chloride.

EXPERIMENT 138—(*Continued*).

What is formed when tin is dissolved in hydrochloric acid?

What other compound of tin and chlorine is there?

[When stannous chloride, $SnCl_2$, acts upon mercuric chloride, $HgCl_2$, the former takes a part or all of the chlorine from the latter, forming either mercurous chloride, $HgCl$, or mercury, according to the relative amounts of the two substances present, thus:

$$2HgCl_2 + SnCl_2 = 2HgCl + SnCl_4;$$
$$HgCl_2 + SnCl_2 = Hg + SnCl_4.]$$

7. Treat the precipitate obtained in the case of the arsenic with 4–5 cubic centimeters of a concentrated solution of ammonium carbonate. To the solution add hydrochloric acid and a few crystals of potassium chlorate, and boil until chlorine is no longer given off. Add ammonia, ammonium chloride, and magnesium sulphate to the solution. [The precipitate is ammonium magnesium arsenate, NH_4MgAsO_4.] Compare Experiment 98a.

8. Dissolve the tin precipitate in dilute hydrochloric acid. Add a few small pieces of zinc. Dissolve in hydrochloric acid the tin which separates.

What will the solution thus obtained contain?

What should take place on adding the solution to a solution of mercuric chloride? Try it.

Mix the solutions prepared in 1, and proceed as follows:

9. Pass hydrogen sulphide until the liquid smells strongly of it (showing that the metals have been completely precipitated as sulphides); filter; wash;

EXPERIMENT 138—(*Continued*).

treat the precipitate with ammonium sulphide ; filter ; wash.

What is now in solution ?

What is in the filter ?

10. Treat the solution with dilute sulphuric acid. Filter ; wash. Treat the precipitate thus obtained with concentrated ammonium carbonate. Filter ; wash. Treat the solution as directed in 7 ; and the precipitate as in 8.

11. Treat with a mixture of warm concentrated nitric and hydrochloric acids the precipitate left after treating with ammonium sulphide as in 9. Test for copper as in 5; and for mercury as in 6.

STUDY OF GROUP III.

ALUMINIUM.

EXPERIMENT 139.

1. Prepare a solution of ordinary alum. [What is ordinary alum?]

2. Add to this solution ammonia, ammonium chloride, and ammonium sulphide. Filter and wash. Treat the precipitate with hydrochloric acid; and then treat the solution thus obtained with ammonium chloride and ammonia.

[Aluminium does not form a sulphide; but the hydroxide, $Al(OH)_3$, is formed when ammonia, ammonium chloride, and ammonium sulphide are added to a solution of its salts. When the hydroxide is treated with hydrochloric acid it is converted into the chloride, $AlCl_3$, which dissolves; and when the solution of the chloride is treated with ammonia the hydroxide is precipitated:

$$AlCl_3 + 3NH_3 + 3H_2O = Al(OH)_3 + 3NH_4Cl.]$$

3. Dissolve the precipitate of aluminium hydroxide, $Al(OH)_3$, in as little hydrochloric acid as possible, and add a cold solution of sodium hydroxide. Boil the solution thus obtained.

4. After cooling slowly add dilute hydrochloric acid. When the alkali is neutralized, aluminium hydroxide, $Al(OH)_3$, will be precipitated. It will dissolve on the addition of more acid; and from the solution thus obtained the hydroxide can be precipitated by a solution of ammonia.

I

CHROMIUM.

EXPERIMENT 140.

1. Prepare a solution of chromic chloride, $CrCl_3$, as directed in Experiment 123*b*.

2. Treat the solution as under 2 and 3, Experiment 139, and note the differences.

How could you distinguish between aluminium and chromium?

IRON.

EXPERIMENT 141.

1. Prepare a solution of ferrous chloride. [See Experiment 119, 1.]

2. Convert a part of this into ferric chloride. [See Experiment 119, 4.]

3. Treat each of these solutions with ammonia and ammonium sulphide.

[The precipitate is the same in both cases, and the action is represented thus:

$$FeCl_2 + (NH_4)_2S = FeS + 2NH_4Cl;$$
$$2FeCl_3 + 3(NH_4)_2S = 2FeS + 6NH_4Cl + S.]$$

4. Dissolve the precipitate in hydrochloric acid.

$$[FeS + 2HCl = FeCl_2 + H_2S.]$$

5. Convert the ferrous into ferric chloride. [See Experiment 119, 4.]

6. Treat with ammonium chloride and ammonia. Filter and wash. Treat the precipitate as directed under 3, Experiment 139.

What differences are there between aluminium, chromium, and iron?

7. Filter; dissolve the precipitate in hydrochloric acid; and treat with a solution of potassium ferrocyanide (yellow prussiate of potash), $K_4Fe(CN)_6$.

ZINC.

EXPERIMENT 142.

1. Prepare a dilute solution of zinc sulphate.
2. Treat with ammonia and ammonium sulphide. What is the color of the precipitate? The composition is ZnS.
3. Dissolve in dilute hydrochloric acid.

$$ZnS + 2HCl = ZnCl_2 + H_2S.$$

4. Treat with ammonium chloride and ammonia. Is a precipitate formed?
5. Add enough hydrochloric acid to give the solution an acid reaction, and then add sodium acetate, $NaC_2H_3O_2$:

$$ZnCl_2 + 2NaC_2H_3O_2 = 2NaCl + Zn(C_2H_3O_2)_2.$$

6. Pass hydrogen sulphide through the solution. The white precipitate is zinc sulphide, ZnS.

What differences are there between aluminium, chromium, iron, and zinc? How could they be separated and detected if present in the same solution?

It will be well for the teacher to prepare solutions containing two or more members of Group III, and to give them to the pupil for analysis.

MANGANESE.

EXPERIMENT 143.

1. Treat a little manganese dioxide in a test-tube with hydrochloric acid. Boil, dilute, and filter.

What have you in solution? [See Experiment 62.]

2. Treat as under 2, 3, 4, 5, 6, in the preceding experiment.

In what respects do manganese and zinc differ?

3. To the solution through which you have just passed hydrogen sulphide add sodium hydroxide, NaOH, until the most of the acetic acid is neutralized; heat gently and add bromine water. Let the liquid stand for an hour.

What takes place? [The composition of the precipitate is represented by the formula $Mn(OH)_4$.]

How could you separate manganese from the other members of the group?

SEPARATION OF ELEMENTS OF GROUP III.

EXPERIMENT 144.

1. Mix dilute solutions of alum, chromic chloride (prepared as in Experiment 123b), ferrous chloride (prepared as in Experiment 119), zinc sulphate, and manganese chloride.

2. Treat with ammonia, ammonium chloride, and ammonium sulphide. Filter and wash.

3. Treat the precipitate with dilute hydrochloric acid; treat with nitric acid to convert ferrous chloride into ferric chloride (Experiment 119, 4); and then treat the solution thus obtained with ammonium chloride and ammonia.

What have you in the precipitate? (Label this A.)
What in the solution? (Label this B.)

4. Dissolve the precipitate in a little dilute hydrochloric acid, and add a cold solution of sodium hydroxide, more than enough to neutralize the hydrochloric acid. Filter; dissolve the precipitate in hydrochloric acid, and treat with a solution of potassium ferrocyanide, $K_4Fe(CN)_6$. [See Experiment 141, 7.] Boil the filtrate from the precipitate of ferric hydroxide. What is precipitated? Treat the filtrate as directed in Experiment 139, 4.

5. Treat the solution B (see under 3 above) as directed under 5 and 6, Experiment 142; and under 3, Experiment 143. Examine mixtures containing members of Group III.

STUDY OF GROUP IV.

CALCIUM.
Experiment 145.

1. Prepare a solution of calcium chloride by dissolving a little calcium carbonate (marble) in hydrochloric acid. What is the reaction?

2. Treat with ammonium chloride, ammonia, and ammonium carbonate, $(NH_4)_2CO_3$. Filter and wash.

What takes place? Write the equation.

3. Dissolve the precipitate in dilute hydrochloric acid. Treat a small part of this solution with a solution of calcium sulphate in water. Treat another small part with ammonia and ammonium oxalate, $(NH_4)_2C_2O_4$. The precipitate is calcium oxalate, CaC_2O_4.

Does a solution of calcium chloride give a precipitate when treated with a solution of calcium sulphate?

BARIUM.

EXPERIMENT 146.

1. Prepare a dilute solution of barium chloride in water.

2. Treat as directed under 2, preceding Experiment.

3. Dissolve the precipitate in dilute hydrochloric acid. Treat a small part of this solution with a solution of calcium sulphate in water.

What difference do you notice between the conduct of calcium and that of barium?

How could you detect barium and calcium when present in the same solution? Mix the solutions of barium and calcium chlorides, and try the reactions described in Experiments 145 and 146.

STUDY OF GROUP V.

MAGNESIUM.

EXPERIMENT 147.

1. Prepare a dilute solution of magnesium sulphate in water.

2. Add ammonium chloride, ammonia, and disodium phosphate, HNa_2PO_4.

The precipitate formed is ammonium magnesium phosphate, NH_4MgPO_4. What similar precipitate has already been obtained? (See Experiment 138, 7.)

3. Mix solutions of barium chloride, calcium chloride, and magnesium chloride, and see whether you can detect the three metals by means of the reactions described in Experiments 145, 146, and 147.

STUDY OF GROUP VI.

EXPERIMENT 148.

1. Potassium can be detected by means of the color it gives to a flame (see Experiment 110), and also by the fact that when chlorplatinic acid, H_2PtCl_6, is added to a solution of a potassium salt, the salt, K_2PtCl_6, is precipitated. (See Experiment 110a.) Try this.

2. Sodium is detected by means of the flame reaction (see Experiment 110).

3. Ammonium salts are detected by adding an alkali, when ammonia gas is given off, and this is easily recognized by its odor or by its action on a moistened piece of red litmus-paper.

GENERAL DIRECTIONS.

By the aid of the reactions thus far studied you will find it possible to analyze substances which contain the following metals either alone or mixed together:

Silver, lead, mercury, copper, tin, arsenic, aluminium, chromium, iron, zinc, manganese, calcium, barium, magnesium, potassium, sodium, and ammonium. After the metals have been detected, the next question to be answered is: In what forms of combination were they present in the original substance taken for analysis? Or, in other words, what salts were present? To answer this question, recall the experiments you have made in the general reactions of chlorides, nitrates, sulphates, and carbonates. These are the most common salts, and, for the present, it will be best to confine your work to these.

CLASSIFICATION OF SUBSTANCES STUDIED.

It will now be well to draw up a table containing the names and symbols of all the substances with which you have had to deal, classifying them into:

(1) *Elements* and *Compounds;*

(2) *Acids*, *Bases*, and *Salts*.

Under *Elements* state the principal source and the principal method for getting each.

Under *Compounds* state the source and the principal method for the preparation of each.

Classify all the compounds you have had to deal with into:

(1) Those which are gaseous;

(2) Those which are liquid;

(3) Those which are solid at the ordinary temperature;

(4) Those solids and liquids which easily undergo change when heated (state what the change is, and give the equation expressing the change).

Classify the compounds further into:

(1) Those which are soluble in water without change;

(2) Those which dissolve in water and are changed (state what the change is, and give the equation expressing the change);

(3) Those which are insoluble in water.

WEIGHTS AND MEASURES.

ENGLISH SYSTEM.

Troy or Apothecaries' Weight.

Pound.		Ounces.		Drams.		Scruples.		Grains.		Grams.
1	=	12	=	96	=	288	=	5760	=	372.96
		1	=	8	=	24	=	480	=	31.08
				1	=	3	=	60	=	3.885
						1	=	20	=	1.295
								1	=	0.0647

Avoirdupois Weight.

Pound.		Ounces.		Drams.		Grains.		Grams.
1	=	16	=	256	=	7000	=	453.25
		1	=	16	=	437.5	=	28.328
				1	=	27.343	=	1.77

Imperial Measure.

Gallon.		Pints.		Fl. Ounces.		Fl. Drams.		Minims.		Cubic Centimeters.
1	=	8	=	160	=	1280	=	76800	=	4545.86
		1	=	20	=	160	=	9600	=	568.23
				1	=	8	=	480	=	28.41
						1	=	60	=	3.55

METRIC SYSTEM.

Measures of Length.

Meter.		Decimeters.		Centimeters.		Millimeters.		Inches.
1	=	10	=	100	=	1000	=	39.87100
		1	=	10	=	100	=	3.93710
				1	=	10	=	0.39371
						1	=	0.03937

Measures of Capacity.

Liter.		Cubic Centimeters.		Pints.		Cubic Inches.
1	=	1000	=	1.76	=	61.0363
		1	=	0.00176	=	0.0610
		16.38			=	1.00

Measures of Weight.

Kilogram.		Grams.		Lbs. (Avoirdupois).		Grains.
1	=	1000	=	2.2046	=	15432.00
		1	=	0.0022	=	15.43

CHEMISTRY

Cairns's Quantitative Chemical Analysis
Revised and enlarged by Dr. E. Waller. 417 pp. 8vo. $2.00, *net*.

Cohen's Physical Chemistry for Biologists
Translated by Dr. Martin Fischer, Chicago University. (*In preparation.*)

Congdon's Qualitative Analysis
By Prof. Ernest A. Congdon, Drexel Institute. 64 pp. Interleaved. 8vo. 60c., *net*.

Nicholson and Avery's Exercises in Chemistry
With Outlines for the Study of Chemistry. To accompany any elementary text. By Prof. H. H. Nicholson, University of Nebraska, and Prof. Samuel Avery, University of Idaho. 413 pp. 12mo. 60c., *net*.

Noyes's (A. A.) General Principles of Physical Science
An Introduction to the Study of the Principles of Chemistry. By Prof. A. A. Noyes, Mass. Institute of Technology. 160 pp. 8vo. $1.50, *net*.

Noyes's (W. A.) Organic Chemistry
By Prof. Wm. A. Noyes, Rose Polytechnic Institute. (*In press.*)

Qualitative Analysis (Elementary)
x + 91 pp. 8vo. 80c., *net*.

Remsen's Chemistries
By Pres. Ira Remsen, Johns Hopkins. (*American Science Series.*)
Inorganic Chemistry (*Advanced*). xxii + 853 pp. 8vo. $2.80, *net*.
College Chemistry xx + 689 pp. 8vo. $2.00, *net*.
Introduction to Chemistry (*Briefer*). xix + 435 pp. 12mo. $1.12, *net*.
This book is used in hundreds of schools and colleges in this country. It has passed through several editions in England, and has been translated into German (being the elementary text-book in the University of Leipsic), French, and Italian.
Remsen and Randall's Experiments (*for the "Introduction"*). 50c., *net*.
Elements of Chemistry (*Elementary*). x + 272 pp. 12mo. 80c., *net*.
Laboratory Manual (*for the "Elements"*). 40c., *net*.

Torrey's Elementary Chemistry
By Joseph Torrey, Jr., Harvard. 437 pp. 12mo. $1.25, *net*.

White's Qualitative Analysis
By Prof. John White, Univ. of Nebraska. 96 pp. 8vo. 80c., *net*.

Woodhull and Van Arsdale's Chemical Experiments
By Prof. John F. Woodhull and M. B. Van Arsdale, Teachers' College, New York City. 136 pp. 12mo. 60c., *net*.
Extremely simple experiments in the chemistry of daily life.

HENRY HOLT & CO. 29 West 23d Street, New York
378 Wabash Avenue, Chicago

BRITTON'S MANUAL OF THE FLORA OF THE NORTHERN STATES AND CANADA.

By Director N. L. BRITTON of the New York Botanical Garden.
1080 pp.   8vo. $2.25, net.

A comprehensive manual of over a thousand pages, containing about 4,500 descriptions, probably one-third more than any other. It is designed to meet modern requirements and outline modern conceptions of the science. It is based on *An Illustrated Flora*, prepared by Prof. Britton in co-operation with Judge Addison Brown. The text has been revised and brought up to date, and much of novelty has been added. All illustrations are omitted, but specific reference has been made to all of the 4,162 figures in the *Illustrated Flora*.

"It is the most complete and reliable work that ever appeared in the form of a flora of this region, and for the first time we have a manual in which the plant descriptions are drawn from the plants themselves, and do not represent compiled descriptions made by the early writers."—Prof. L. M. Underwood of Columbia.

"This work will at once take its place as the standard manual of the region that it covers. It is far superior to any other work of its class ever published in America."—Prof. Conway MacMillan of University of Minnesota.

"This book must at once find its way into the schools and colleges, to which it may be commended for the students in systematic botany."—Prof. Chas. E. Bessey in "Science."

"It is nothing if it is not compact; it is nothing if it is not up to date; it is nothing if it is not the work of a master. What more can be said, save that the more it is used the greater the appreciation by the plant-lovers in the region which it covers."—Prof. Byron D. Halsted of Rutgers College.

"The work is well done; and as it is the only volume which gives in a way suitable for students the present state of the science, it cannot fail to take its place as a standard work."—Prof. George Macloskie of Princeton.

"I regard the book as one that we cannot do without and one that will henceforth take its place as a necessary means of determination of the plant species within its range."—Prof. V. M. Spalding of University of Michigan.

"An exceedingly valuable contribution to our botanical literature. . . . It is convenient to handle, and the low price will help to give it a large circulation."—Prof. T. J. Burrill of the University of Illinois.

HENRY HOLT & CO., 29 West 23d Street, New York
378 Wabash Avenue, Chicago

SCIENCE TEXT-BOOKS AND WORKS OF REFERENCE.

All prices are NET *unless marked* RETAIL. *Details of the books will be found in Henry Holt & Co.'s Educational Catalogue, free on application.*

American Science Series

Physics. By Prof. GEORGE F. BARKER, University of Pennsylvania.
   Advanced Course. 902 pp. 8vo. $3.50
Chemistry. By Prest. IRA REMSEN, Johns Hopkins University.
   Chemistry. *Advanced Course.* 850 pp. 8vo.   2.80
   College Chemistry. xx + 669 pp. 8vo.   2.00
   Chemistry. *Briefer Course.* (*New Edition*, 1901.) 435 pp. 12mo. 1.10
   Chemistry. *Elementary Course.* 272 pp. 12mo.   80c.
   Laboratory Manual (*to Elementary Course*). 196 pp. 12mo.   40c.
   Chemical Experiments. By Prof. REMSEN and Dr. W. W. RANDALL. (*For Briefer Course.*) No blank pages for notes. 158 pp. 12mo.   50c.
Astronomy. By Prof. SIMON NEWCOMB of Johns Hopkins and EDWARD S. HOLDEN, late Director of the Lick Observatory, California.
   Advanced Course. 512 pp. 8vo.   2.00
   The same. *Briefer Course.* 352 pp. 12mo.   1.12
   The same. *Elementary Course.* By E. S. HOLDEN, 446 pp. 12mo. 1.20
Geology. By Profs. THOMAS C. CHAMBERLAIN and ROLLIN D. SALISBURY, University of Chicago. (*In preparation.*)
General Biology. By Prof. W. T. SEDGWICK, Mass. Institute of Technology, and Prof. E. B. WILSON, Columbia Univ. *Revised and Enlarged.* 231 pp. 8vo.   1.75
Botany. By Prof. C. E. BESSEY, Univ. of Nebraska.
   Advanced Course. 611 pp. 8vo.   2.20
   The same. *Briefer Course.* 356 pp.   1.12
Zoology. By Prof. A. S. PACKARD, Jr., Brown University.
   Advanced Course. 722 pp. 8vo.   2.40
   The same. *Briefer Course.* 338 pp.   1.12
   The same. '*Elementary Course.* 290 pp. 12mo.   80c.
The Human Body. By H. NEWELL MARTIN, sometime professor in the Johns Hopkins University.
   Advanced Course. 685 pp. 8vo. (Copies without chapter on Reproduction sent when specially ordered.)   2.50
   The same. *Briefer Course.* (*Entirely new edition, revised by Prof. G. Wells Fitz of Harvard.*) 408 pp. 12mo.   1.20
   The same. *Elementary Course.* 261 pp. 12mo.   75c.
   The Human Body and the Effects of Narcotics. 261 pp. 12mo. 1.20
Psychology. By Prof. WILLIAM JAMES of Harvard.
   Advanced Course. 689 + 704 pp. 8vo. 2 vols.   4.80
   The same. *Briefer Course.* 478 pp. 12mo.   1.60
Ethics. By Profs. JOHN DEWEY and JAMES H. TUFTS, Chicago University. (*In preparation.*)
Political Economy. By the late President FRANCIS A. WALKER, Mass., Institute of Technology.
   Advanced Course. 537 pp. 8vo.   2.00
   The same. *Briefer Course.* 415 pp. 12mo.   1.20
   The same. *Elementary Course.* 423 pp. 12mo.   1.00
Finance. By Prof. HENRY CARTER ADAMS, University of Michigan.
   Advanced Course. 573 pp. 8vo.   2.50

Henry Holt & Co.'s Works on Science

Allen's Laboratory Exercises in Elementary Physics. By CHAS. R. ALLEN of the New Bedford, Mass., High School. 209 pp. (Teachers' Edition, $1.) *Pupils' Edition*, 80c.

Arthur, Barnes, and Coulter's Handbook of Plant Dissection. By Prof. J. C. ARTHUR, Purdue University, Prof. C. R. BARNES, and Prof. JOHN M. COULTER, Chicago University. 256 pp. $1.20

Atkinson's Elementary Botany. By Prof. GEO. F. ATKINSON, Cornell Univ. *Fully Illustrated.* 441 pp. 1.25

—— **Lessons in Botany.** *Illustrated.* 365 pp. 1.12

Barnes's Plant Life. By Prof. C. R. BARNES, University of Chicago. *Illustrated.* 428 pp. 1.12

—— **Outlines of Plant Life.** *Illustrated.* 308 pp. 1.00

Beal's Grasses of North America. For Farmers and Students. By Prest. W. J. BEAL, Michigan Agricultural College. Copiously illustrated. 8vo.; Vol. I, 457 pp., $2.50. Vol. II, 707 pp., 5.00

Britton's Manual of the Flora of the Northern States and Canada. By Director N. L. BRITTON of N. Y. Botanical Gardens. 1080 pp. 2.25

Bumpus's Laboratory Course in Invertebrate Zoology By Prof. H. C. BUMPUS, Brown University. Revised. 157 pp. 1.00

Cairns's Quantitative Chemical Analysis. By FRED'K A. CAIRNS. Revised and edited by Dr. E. WALLER. 417 pp. 8vo. 2.00

Cohen's Physical Chemistry for Biologists. Translated by Dr. MARTIN H. FISCHER, University of Chicago. [*In preparation.*]

Congdon's Qualitative Analysis. By Prof. ERNEST A. CONGDON of Drexel Institute. 64 pp. Interleaved. 8vo. 60c.

Crozier's Dictionary of Botanical Terms. 202 pp. 8vo. 2.40

Ganong's Laboratory Course in Plant Physiology. By Prof. W. F. GANONG, Smith College. vi + 147 pp. 8vo. 1.00

Hackel's The True Grasses. Translated from " Die natürlichen Pflanzenfamilien." 228 pp. 8vo. 1.50

Hall's First Lessons in Experimental Physics. By Prof. EDWIN H. HALL, Harvard Univ. 120 pp 12mo. 65c.

Hall's and Bergen's Text-book of Physics. By Prof. EDWIN H. HALL, and JOSEPH Y. BERGEN, Jr., Junior Master in the English High School, Boston. *Greatly enlarged edition.* 596 pp. 12mo. 1.25

Hertwig's Text-book of Zoology. Translated by Prof. J. S. KINGSLEY of Tufts College. *With over 650 illustrations.* (Oct. '02.)

—— **General Principles of Zoology.** *Being Part 1 of the above.* Translated and edited by Prof. G. WILTON FIELD. 226 pp. 8vo. 1.60

Howell's Dissection of the Dog. As a Basis for the Study of Physiology. By Prof. W. H. HOWELL of Johns Hopkins. 100 pp. 8vo. 1.00

Jackman's Nature Study for the Common Schools. (Arranged by the Months.) By WILBUR JACKMAN of the Cook County Normal School, Chicago, Ill. 448 pp. 1.20

Jordan's Guide to Fishes. By Prest. DAVID STARR JORDAN, Stanford Univ. *Fully Illustrated.* (*In press.*)

Kellogg's First Lessons in Zoology. By Prof. V. L. KELLOGG, Stanford Univ. (*In press.*)

—— **Elements of Zoology.** *Revised Edition.* 484 pp. 1.20

Henry Holt & Co.'s Works on Science

Kerner and Oliver's Natural History of Plants. Translated by Prof. F. W. OLIVER of University College, London. 4to. 4 parts. With over 1000 illustrations and 16 colored plates. $15.00

Kingsley's Vertebrate Zoology. By Prof. J. F. KINGSLEY, Tufts College. Illustrated. 439 pp. 8vo. 3.00

— **Elements of Comparative Zoology.** 347 pp. 12mo. 1.20

Macalister's Zoology of the Invertebrate and Vertebrate Animals. By ALEX. MACALISTER. Revised by A. S. PACKARD. 277 pp. 16mo. 80c.

Macloskie's Elementary Botany. With Students' Guide. By GEORGE MACLOSKIE, D. Sc., LL.D. 373 pp. 1.30

MacMillan's Plant Embryology. By Prof. CONWAY MACMILLAN, University of Minnesota. (In preparation.)

McMurrich's Text-book of Invertebrate Morphology. By Prof. J. PLAYFAIR MCMURRICH, University of Cincinnati. 661 pp. 8vo. New Ed. 3.00

McNab's Botany. Outlines of Morphology, Physiology, and Classification of Plants. By W. RAMSAY MCNAB. Revised by Prof. C. E. BESSEY. 400 pp. 80c.

Merriam's Mammals of the Adirondack Region. By Dr. C. HART MERRIAM. 316 pp. 8vo. 3.50

Nicholson and Avery's Exercises in Chemistry. By Prof. H. H. NICHOLSON, Univ. of Nebraska, and Prof. S. AVERY, Univ. of Idaho. 134 pp. 60c.

Noel's Buz; the Life and Adventures of a Honey Bee. 134 pp. Retail, 1.00

Noyes's, (A. A.), General Principles of Physical Science. An Introduction to the Study of the Principles of Chemistry. By Prof. A. A. NOYES, Mass. Institute of Technology. 160 pp. 8vo. 1.50

Noyes's (W. A.), Elements of Qualitative Analysis. By Prof. WILLIAM A. NOYES, of the Rose Polytechnic Institute. 91 pp. 8vo. 88c.

— **Organic Chemistry.** (Sept. '02.)

Packard's Entomology for Beginners. By A. S. PACKARD. xvi+367 pp. Third Edition Revised. 1.40

— **Guide to the Study of Insects,** and a Treatise on those Injurious and Beneficial to Crops. For Colleges, Farm-Schools, and Agriculturists. With 15 plates and 670 wood-cuts. Ninth Edition. 715 pp. 8vo. 5.00

— **Outlines of Comparative Embryology.** Illustrated. 243 pp. 8vo. 2.50

Peabody's Laboratory Exercises in Anatomy and Physiology. By JAS. EDWARD PEABODY of the Peter Cooper High School, New York. 79 pp. Interleaved. 12mo. 60c.

Percival's Agricultural Botany. By Prof. JOHN PERCIVAL, Southeastern Agricultural College, Wye, England. 798 pp. 12 mo. 2.50

Perkins's Outlines of Electricity and Magnetism. By Prof. CHAS. A. PERKINS, University of Tennessee. 277 pp. 12mo. 1.10

Pierce's Plant Physiology. By Prof. G. J. PIERCE, Stanford Univ. (In press.)

Pierce's Problems of Elementary Physics. Chiefly numerical. By E. DANA PIERCE of the Hotchkiss School. 194 pp. 60c.

viii '02   3